SINGLE, AGAIN

ELLEN HILDEBRAND

FOREWORD

I have this image in my mind, of a woman I don't know. I can feel her presence as my fingers dance across my keyboard. My words are her words. My thoughts are her thoughts. She wonders, "Did I write this myself?" And "How does she know?" That woman, whose face is blurred by the tears we both share, is the reason. She is the reason I opened my heart and my soul.

I have this image of a woman, who I did not think I knew. She is broken in the way that a mirror shatters, but all of the pieces stay intact. I close my eyes and begin to feel my way to her, reaching out with my hands in the darkness. All of the pieces are there, intact, and healed by love, acceptance, and tremendous kindness.

I had this image of a woman I wanted to be. She is strong and confident. She loves with all her heart, freely and without hesitation. She has the courage of a lion and the wings of a swan. Her mission is to take everything she learned and reach you.

This intimate journal is my gift to your gentle heart.

To the four pillars of my life, I dedicate this book to you.

My three sons…

Billy, for giving me direction. Your very existence is the map of my life.

Ricky, for being my sun. I am blessed by the warmth of your love, and the glow of the optimism that is you. You light my way.

My Jack, for being my boat. God knew I would need you, my partner in all things. My warrior.

And my Neil. You are the love of my life. I owe this book to you, for being the story and giving me the courage to print it. You're my everything. And we're just gettin' started.

SINGLE, AGAIN

Nantasket Beach, Massachusetts

2018

My Dear Friend,

It was at the exact moment I recognized my life has a Purpose that I could see how nothing that happened around me was an accident. Discovering my sense of purpose, seeing that there is so much more to this life than what is on the surface, is a gift. A gift that found its way to me when I was lost. Imagine the darkest night, not a star in the sky, when suddenly the sun appears on the horizon. Slowly the sun is all you see, and as it rises to its place in the sky, you realize the darkness was meant to be. I started to ask, "Why am I here?" And then, "What am I supposed to be learning?"

Along the way I have been given the hand of many wonderful souls. Some will be with me forever, and some passed by like a whisper. None by accident, all by design. Their hands made the lessons of my life meaningful, in their touch I discovered Gratitude.

One day I decided I wanted to write my story. I started a blog about the journey of a woman who found herself single, again, at 50. This book is an intimate journal of my perception of my marriage, my divorce, and the healing process that followed. Please know I wrote this from a place of hope. I believe in love and all that comes wrapped inside its beauty. I honor trust, companionship, romance, dignity, and honesty. I recognize that people make mistakes, and I believe in forgiveness as a way to let go of the burden of the past. And most of all, I believe in me.

This will never be a story of what happened to me, that is a chapter. The story is about what I did with what happened to me. I had to find the courage to know that what is ahead of me is my story. And it's definitely a love story.

With love,
Ellen

2010

Terror fills her as she races to the door and throws her body at it. There is an arm inside the house, and she pushes with every ounce of physical and emotional energy to keep the stranger out. The children are inside. Her babies. "Get out, get out, get out!" This is her home to protect. "You don't belong here!!!" She sees the arm reaching inside, trying to grab her and make its way into the house. From the core of her soul she yells, "NO!!! Please, someone help me!!"

His hand is on her arm and she is sitting up in her bed. Her heart is pounding. For a moment, she doesn't know where she is.

"You were screaming" he said.

She falls back, the relief of being awake, still drifting up the stairs...from that front door...where the truth of the dream haunts her. "I had a dream."

"Oh my God," he says. "I've ruined you."

2014

The road was familiar in the way that a distant memory creeps in when you are doing something simple, like laundry. And then suddenly you hear your grandmothers voice and her face is behind your blink, as your hands fold a towel, a T-shirt. There are very few cars on 691 as she enters Meriden. Over her right shoulder is the Meriden Square. A giggle escapes her, and she says out loud… "Meriden Square" …knowing the name has changed decades ago. They grew up shopping there, running around with friends, eating bagels and laughing at Spencer's. And then in college she would come home and find her mother working there. She would come out of the stock room, six pair of shoes in her right arm, a sling back hanging off her pinky. "Hey El", she would say, and then her mother would sell them all. Across the room she sees her sister in her white Clinique coat, surrounded by beautiful girls with perfect hair and mascara, perfect in a way she could never imagine being. Her memories were of G Fox…which became Filene's… and is now Macy's. She drove past the exit, drove by the memory. Never in all of her years did she think she would come back to find a version of herself she left behind, never imagined needing her.

Her car drifted to the end of the exit. Was she really here? She took a left onto Route 10 and headed back into her childhood. She would find her here somewhere. A quick glimpse in the rear-view mirror, and a silent prayer.

"25-year-old me, I need to find you so that you can bring me home." And the light turned green.

Single, Me
November 1

Dear 25-year-old me,

I love watching you in my mind's eye because you are so young, carefree, and fun. You live in the moment, you trust everyone and everything, and you truly believe you control the universe. A full-time job, a part time job, and you never miss a day at the gym. My heart soars as you run effortlessly from one side of town to the other. As busy as you are, you never look up and down the road of your future. Life is a party, and you don't even have to commit to one hair color.

Soon, life for you is going to change dramatically. I smile when I watch you because you don't see it coming. You just added a graduate degree to your already crazy schedule...and you're dating someone new. How do you fit it all in?

Keep smiling single girl.

Love,

Me

Single Again,
November 2

It was easy, not simple, being 25. I clearly remember right before my birthday taking a moment to say goodbye to the child in me. It felt like the right thing to do, and then I continued down the path of "I have no idea where I'm going." I loved it. I had a full-time job by day, a part time job at night, and a passion for running.

Running would become my savior, I just didn't know it yet.

Single Again
November 3

Dear 26-year-old me,

    I am watching you the day he walked into your life, his baseball uniform covered in dirt, his friends, rowdy with excitement at the win. His eyes followed you as you worked, so you smiled and asked about his sister. It's a small town and she had been your friend since first grade. But not him, he was quiet and shy, and really made you uncomfortable. I still laugh when I hear you say, "Fine, I will go out with you, so you can get over me."

    Oh, single girl....

Single Again
November 5

Single girl...you were funny. I don't remember thinking it at the time. It all felt so normal! The first date quickly turned to a second and then a third. He wasn't like the others. He was quirky and difficult in a moody way. The last relationship broke your heart, and while you liked him, deep inside this felt safe. He was not going to break your heart.

Time will teach you to expect things from love. Expect to feel special, treasured, and even cherished. What you didn't know then, single girl, is you began to lower your desires and keep your needs silent. I want to yell on the top of my lungs, so every single girl can hear me......

"Love does not make you feel ashamed of who you are!"

I am watching you get out of his car and I am so very proud of you. He had been screaming at you to tell him how many men you had been with before him. You made up a number, turned and said, "You need to go home and see if you can live with what I just told you. This is on you, I'm fine with me." Yes!!!! It wasn't until you were married that you told him the truth.

You are perfect, single girls, just as you are.

Single Again
November 6

The Power of asking "Why?"

The purpose of my writing this is not to bash a man. I have nothing to gain from that. What matters to me is the transformation of who I was as a young, single girl to who I became when I found myself single, again. What happened, why, and how I let it. No one goes into marriage thinking it might end…and yet 50% do. Suddenly half of us wake up, like I did, wondering how to fix what just happened? Not just to the structure of your life, but to the fabric of who you are.

The last time I was single, I was 26 years old. My view of myself, the world, relationships, everything around me, was through the eyes of innocence. Pretending changed me. Pretending denied me my true self. Suddenly I wanted to feel that free spirit again, I wanted to believe that I hadn't lost myself in the process.

I had developed a new sense of innocence at 48. It was time to get real. I wanted to feel the joy I felt as single me, but only if it was genuine.

Single, Again
November 6

Dearest 26-year-old me,

You are in the bathroom staring at a stick with a pink line. You're shocked, yes, but in your heart, you know that this baby is meant for you. Already you love him, already you are one. This is the moment that changes your life. This is the moment of purpose, of meaning, of direction for you. There is a person coming into this world who will depend on you for everything.

You leave for work and come back to a bouquet of roses and a note: Marry me....

First you chose the baby. Then you chose the man. You chose from the heart and I am proud of you.

Keep smiling Single Girl,
Me

Single, Again
November 7

The first time I got in trouble was for cutting an apple on his kitchen counter. I said, "I'm more worried about my apple than your counter." He lived in a two-story rental above an elderly couple he hoped would leave him their inheritance. At first, I thought he was kidding. Shortly after the stick turned pink, I was informed, "My mother had a certain way of taking care of me, and I'm not sure you'll be able to do that." I should have walked out. My instant reply, "I will make you ashamed of your mother," did not change the way his comment made me feel. My responses were always fueled with sarcasm, a competitive edge, and what appeared to be inner-strength.

The truth is, he was chipping away at me. I was the perfect victim because I responded. What is critical is not what another person does, but how you respond. You can't deny your true response. Listen to your inner voice. Hear what your heart and soul are telling you. Know that making excuses for bad behavior or denying how you feel is not part of a healthy you.

Love craves your honesty. When you feel pain, Love should heal. When you are lost, Love should encourage. Love is the single thing in life with any true value. Think about this: If love is a glowing ball of energy and it comes into your life, it should make you explode with happiness!!! The light of love makes us glow.

Once the seeds of doubt and shame were planted, all he had to do was water them.

Single, Again
November 8

"Dear 27-year-old me,

Two hours after your birthday passed, the greatest gift of your life was placed in your arms. To think you understood what it meant to live?!? Silly girl, life began today...real life, meaningful life. I am watching you dance with your baby boy nestled against your neck, singing softly, and I know you've just fallen in love. The warmth of his little body, the smell of his skin, his fingers wrapped around your pinky.

I will never fail you, baby boy.

I love you,
Mom

Single, Again
November 9

Becoming a parent was the happiest shedding of "selfish me" I could imagine. I lost myself in their version of fun, and what made them happy filled my heart with joy. I really found "my people" in my children. Because of them I flourished, I loved and was loved unconditionally. We were an adorable family, and if I squinted just right…I was happily married.

By our 8th Anniversary we had three children and had lived in 4 homes in 3 different states. Packing, unpacking, and adjusting to a new community became a way of life. From the outside looking in, we looked perfect.

Perfect came with a price.

Single, Again
November 13

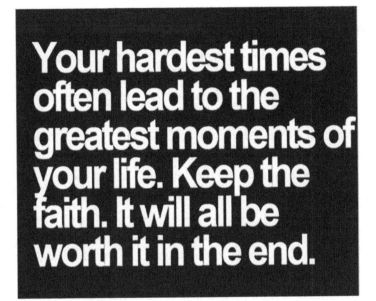

Your hardest times often lead to the greatest moments of your life. Keep the faith. It will all be worth it in the end.

Single, Again
November 13

Dear 27-year-old me,

I want you to go to the mirror and stare at yourself. I want you to look deeply into your eyes, straight into your soul and ask yourself a simple question. "Whose life is this?" Is it yours? And if the answer is yes, I want you to set yourself free in the world and cherish your existence in it. Celebrate you!!! I want you to look at what you have done with the last two years and I want you to be proud of the mother you are and the way you love. Why are you so terrified of failing?

You walk to the mirror and slowly look up. I want to tell you there is no way for you to fail. Listen to my voice, not his. Listen to the laughter of the children, the warmth of their hugs. I need you to know that love is patient, love is kind, and love does not criticize.

This is your life, this is your life, this is your life…
And you're going to be fine.
Love,
Me

Single, Again
November 20

The truth is, I knew right away that I had made a mistake I could not undo. The wedding was beautiful, but as it ended, he got angry. There was a bill he did not want to pay, and the man was standing at the door waiting. I had no money with me and we had agreed ahead of time it was our responsibility to pay this fee.

My sister-in-law suggested we go through the cards we had received as gifts. A bride opening envelopes? Why didn't I insist he pay? There was no fight, there was the tearing of envelopes, there was embarrassment and shock. Until he was ready. He walked up as if nothing had happened, paid the DJ, and gave a handsome tip. A young woman, in a white dress, desperately trying to return cards to their proper envelopes…why? I did not ask, I gathered my things to leave.

It was a beautiful December night and snow was falling gently on the ground. I felt a chill down my spine as we walked to the car. Our best man saw what I felt in words trapped in my throat. He opened the door…to the front seat…and let me sit alone in the back. I was treated to silence for a crime I didn't commit. Why didn't I cry?

I knew then. I knew with every inch of my body. I made a terrible mistake. But I would not quit, I would not fail.

Single, Again

I chase you down the aisle of the church because there is something important, I desperately want you to know. Listen to me, single girl, let me be the voice in your head. Let me assure you that you are doing the right thing. I love that you are proud of your choice, that you are proud of the baby you will one day adore with every inch of your being.

In this moment, you are right. There is love at the end of this aisle, there is pride, and there will be joy. Somewhere, black and white create shades of gray. There will be for better or for worse, in good times and bad, in sickness and in health. You will learn from this marriage and you will fall deeply in love with three gifts from God. It will be worth it.

I'm chasing you...to tell you something else....

Single, Again
November 24

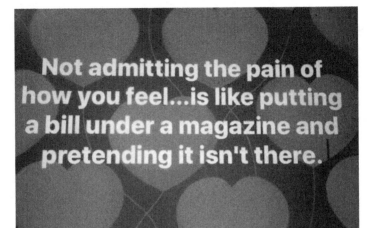

Single, Again
November 25

2016

    I am making a wish and blowing it into my future....

Single, Again
November 25

Dear 32-year-old me,

Here's what I love...

You are in the final mile of the Honolulu Marathon. It's your first marathon, and as you see the finish line you start to cry. There is no way to separate cancer from your run. The little boy that spoke at the Leukemia Society dinner the night before defined every step of the race. When he yelled, "I love my nurse! I love my mom!", there wasn't a dry eye in the room. We could feel his compassion and gratitude, and in this moment, we were part of it. A banquet room filled with runners seeking to make a difference in his life and those like him facing mortality.

Our time here is precious. Every step you take, no matter the direction, is imprinted in a world that needs love.

I look from above and I see your footprints in the sand, across the grass, on the sidewalk, in the road, and on the hearts of people you will never meet.

And your sons...waiting home for their mama.

Love,
Me

Single, Again
November 25

What would Perfect look like…if it were Real?

Single, Again
November 27

Marriage is a funny little institution because what makes it so uniquely amazing is what makes it difficult for a couple. Difficult, but not impossible: Growing a family. It's not the stress, it's the focus. I'll be the first to admit, my eyes turned to my son...and so did his. We adored this boy with every fiber of our being. The sleepless nights, the feedings, the bathing, the diapers, and the rocking, became the norm. Life became a blend of the chaos and joy of growing a family. Two years later I would fall in love again, as would he, with our second son.

By its very nature, a growing family, grows. Houses get bigger, cars turn into minivans, and schedules become more demanding. Time flies by.

I woke up one day and realized my heart no longer fit in my body and spilled out everywhere I looked. I had three sons and I was packing to move to our fifth home.

I was so busy I didn't see the unraveling. I knew deep inside I was lonely. I never asked for more. I never expected more. I just smiled and kept going. I believed that the best way to keep him from hurting me was to have no expectations. If I didn't want anything, he couldn't let me down. I believed if I never said out loud what I was feeling inside, I could not fail.

The truth is that love should come with expectations. I should have recognized my heartbeat, my worth.

The problem is who you become when you start believing you aren't worth anything.

Single, Again
November 28

I believe the world would be a much better place if women had more respect for women.

Single, Again
November 29

I wonder what it was like for someone who had known me my whole life to look at me morph into Married Me? I travel back to 1997 to look for myself.

I am peeking through the window of house number 2 and there you are, ignoring all the signs. Married girl with the perfectly vacuumed carpet, the house without dust or dirt. I look at you Married Girl, and it isn't what you are doing that makes me sad. You have spent the entire day making sure that the home looks unlived in, unaltered by the little people that race around you. Why are you trying to prove that you are worthy of Motherhood? You live in fear of someone entering your home and finding a flaw. Why? And then you remember why.

Brace yourself, Married Girl, he will find the one thing you didn't do perfectly. It's just a house, just a car, just money, just things - useless things.

The sound of his car coming down the driveway catches my attention. The door opens, the end of his day, the beginning of yours. He climbs the stairs, points and says in The Voice, "What is that????? What is that SPOT on the carpet???" You freeze and turn, wanting to throw your body over the small spot you never saw. I want to climb through the window and scoop you up, but it's too soon.

Years from now, he will tell you your two greatest flaws. He sees women picking up their husbands' dry cleaning and he has to clear his own dinner plate. You turn and ask, "Why would you want me to do that when you can?"

But he doesn't hear you. He can't hear you...he's not listening.

Single, Again
November 30

Seven years into our marriage we were relocated to a small town in Wisconsin, half a country from everyone I knew. Every morning he woke up and drove to an office with the same people, following the same career. Getting into the car with the kids before GPS was an interesting challenge because I never knew if I could get us back home. We would all cheer as I pulled up the driveway. Then I would quickly bless myself.

We were starting over. Again.

The choices I made for myself were externally good ones. I gave a lot of my time to the children's school, an unbelievable amount of time, and I loved it. Being an active mom was rewarding and being busy kept me distracted. Our house was breathtaking, and as we got used to the community, my kids began to flourish. Hockey, baseball, football, lots of friends and laughter.

Running would be my solace, my joy, my escape. I love the way the brain expands and travels through thought patterns I don't know I have until I run. Early on I coined that My Runners Brain. Running taught me to deal with only where my foot was at that moment. If there was a hill up the road, I should see it and recognize it is there, and then return my focus to where I am. I could never deal with the hill until I was on it. I began training for my second marathon. There were days I would run ten miles on the treadmill while the kids played around me, then headed outside for the second ten. The day of the marathon I stood at the center of the pack with my neighbor who was running the half marathon with her husband. We were less than a mile from our home, in a beautiful park by the lake. The length of the race, I never once worried where I was or what my time was. I just ran. Suddenly I was approaching the finish line, with people cheering and a great big clock overhead. My name was announced, and my time. My husband wrapped me in a silver blanket and hugged me. "I think I just qualified for Boston", I said through my tears. He shook his head and said, "I knew you were going to. I was following your pace the whole way."

The next day my best friend called me screaming, "OH MY GOD! Go get your newspaper!!" We were both new to the community and she was even more excited than me to see my name on the front page of the newspaper and the sports page. I had always wondered what it would be like to be one of the people that won? What it would be like to set the record? Win the award? I learned that it did not matter whether I was first or last. I believe that every time you think of something you want to do, you should do it. Don't worry about the outcome. Just do it. Participate in life. You never want to be left with a bucket full of ideas you never had the courage to test.

Single Again
December 1

We lived in Wisconsin for three years. Silently the community weaved itself into my being. Friends became family. I was honored with a God Daughter. My job was rewarding, and my children were in a school I wish I could bottle. It was one of those places that you can't believe is real. I was living a life of gratitude.

I have very few memories of him during those years. We lived side by side, peacefully, like railroad tracks without a train. And while I was thinking he was so lucky to have the life I provided, I was kidding myself. I was not his partner, his love, the woman he cared for and shared life with. The world for him existed outside.

He arranged a job transfer behind my back. Suddenly we were moving. Again.

I could hear my heart break as it hit the floor.

Single, Again
December 9

Dear me, Dear you,

Take your right hand and hold your left. Let your fingers drift between each other and allow yourself to feel. You are a unique individual, different than every other on Earth, and this is how it is meant to be.

You are valuable. Incredibly valuable and eternally worthy.

Live from the inside out. Ask your soul why you are here and answer with your actions.

You are important.

Each and every step you take is meaningful and touches those around you.

Make no mistake, you are the author of your own story.

Dear me, Dear you,

Do not pass the pen of your story to another.

Do not turn your head to a mirror and use another's eyes.

Look. See. Know.

Place your head gently on your pillow. Thank the universe for this chance. Allow your arms to fall firmly across you and hug the body that carries your heart and soul.

And drift off to sleep.

Please....Don't wake up one day and wonder who you are.

Single, Again
December 10
2010

Dear Him,

The door opens, like clockwork, and you enter. You go to the sink and wash your hands. Three paper towels. Every time. The mail neatly stacked on the counter. Your dinner plate perfectly placed on the table. Children. A family arranged around a table like a painting.

What was it like? Watching me after the day I found her letter? How did it feel to watch me wither away, knowing I was dying inside? Knowing that my life, my family, the safety of my children, their happiness and security, was slipping through my fingers?

What was that like? Wondering how much I weighed? Kissing your children goodnight. Did you feel anything? At all?

Wondered,
Her

Single, Again
December 11

Clouds. The sun peeking out behind a dusty pile of fluffy white. Your breathing is coming faster, but you need this. The pounding of your feet against the pavement, one foot in front of the other...one foot, one foot. The air is trapped, your lungs are closing until you can't breathe. Your brain asks, "How can this be? Running is your savior?"

One foot, in front, of the other, don't stop, don't let this win.

You realize, in the middle of a panic attack, that the person who created this state for you is somewhere happy. He has it all. He has a wife racing around trying to keep her family whole. He has a girlfriend, with voids in her life, using him to make her whole. He has it all, or so it appears to him at the time.

You realize...that the state of your thoughts is in your control and possession.

You realize...that every thought has a corresponding physical reaction, a racing heart, terror, and sadness.

You realize.... you have done nothing wrong, hurtful, or dishonest.

You accept that only you can stop the pain.

You formulate a plan of survival. With a pencil and scrap paper you create the "Dark Forest", a place where your brain goes, and your body reacts.

And you vow never to go there again.

Single, Again
December 12

Dear me,

 You were tested.

 Someone made you question: Are you worthy? Are you lovable?

 Someone made you wonder: Are you capable? Of life without him?

 Someone made you feel: ugly, undesirable, useless?

 You were tested.

 You questioned, you wondered, and you felt…but did you believe?

 And then suddenly, a hand appeared out of nowhere. And the desire to grab it was overwhelming.

Single, Again
December 14

The rules of the Dark Forest meant that I had to control my thoughts. It wasn't easy, and sometimes I found myself racing through the center of the forest never realizing I had entered. Where were they having sex? What was I going to come home to hear? I became vigilante in my awareness of when my world became dark. The second I noticed my mind drifting, I sang out loud. Speak. Yell. Laugh. Cough. Jump up and down. Scream. I had catch phrases and songs that I would belt out to change the pattern of my thoughts. Try singing "It's raining men" and focusing on anything other than "Hallelujah!"

From the time I found her first letter until the moment I had the courage to leave was roughly five years. Those five years were the hardest of my life. I want you to know that if someone is hurting you …

1. You don't have to be silent about it. People will still love you.

2. Leaving a relationship doesn't mean you failed. It's ok to choose you.

3. Your mind and heart and body are precious gifts…treat them as such. Don't let someone's treatment of you define your self-esteem or self-vision. The other person can be wrong.

4. We make mistakes when we say, "I do" because sometimes "I don't".

5. "For better or for worse" does not mean that you have vowed to tolerate abuse. It means that whatever the world throws at you, you will survive together, NOT whatever one person throws at the other.

6. Love feels good. Love feels happy. Love makes you proud. If you had to buy love, it would retail at millions of dollars per ounce.

But when it's right…it's free.

Single, Again
December 15

Dear me in mid-crisis,

It's 10:00 am and you walk into the bathroom to get ready for work. He follows you in, stops and looks at your reflection in the mirror.

I want to race into the room and cover your ears, block his mouth, pull you from what's about to be said. I couldn't help you then, but I can today. He looks at you and says,

"It's too bad no one has ever loved you, not even your parents."

"That's not true, people have loved me."

"Please, none of your old boyfriends ever loved you."

A cannon blew a hole through the center of me, and I realize I can't breathe when a sound in the hallway lets me know my son heard the entire conversation.

Single, Again
December 16

The train is full of people heading to Boston, each of us going our separate ways when we get off, but in this moment, we are all together. Looking out the window I see towns rushing by me, swimming pools covered for the season as summer turns to fall.

He doesn't know my plan. He doesn't understand that the job I have accepted is a key to my freedom. He doesn't believe I will ever have the courage to leave.

And neither do I.

Single, Again
December 17

It's true...nothing tied me to him. I wasn't in "prison", I was in "a family". I was a wife. So why didn't I walk? Was he holding me there or was I holding myself?

I think about Single Girl growing up in a small town with an average amount of drama and an overdose of silliness. It is amazing how we are defined by our groups...our family, our friends and teammates, the people we work with. For as much as we want to see ourselves as Individuals, we are also the product of how we are affected by our groups. Did my parents love me? Did my siblings include me? Was I accepted by my peers? Would I win a race? Get a job? Be a success?

What happens around us, what is said and what is done, affects how we perceive ourselves in the world. It takes a disciplined mind to stay out of the Dark Forest, and to be the master of our own mind and perception.

The problem with the Dark Forest is that we don't always know we need the discipline until it's too late. Messages are delivered subtly, changes happen slowly, and we deny the insults and the hurts. We pretend we aren't morphing into the person who....

We don't know anymore.

Single, Again
December 18

A lesson from Jack.

"It isn't what Jack tells Jill that matters. It's what Jill tells Jill when Jack stops talking." - Jack Canfield

The Journey

You're walking down the beach, eyes glazing over the bouquet of shells and stones, hoping to find a treasure. Suddenly, you stop and turn to the ocean, and pause. My God, it's so beautiful. How did you forget to look at it? For several moments, you stand still and soak it in.

Life is like that. Every so often you have to stop and look at what you've done. And honor it.

Single, Again
December 20

Memories

It was the summer of 1981....

The Copper Valley gang...swimming, tennis, cards, back to the pool.... laughing all day, secret crushes, Cheetos, the water ballet show. The scent of chlorine permeating every item you own. This is what friends do: They light off fireworks in your heart, braid your hair, race you down the pool in practice, and cheer for you in meets. Whispering into the phone, crying over heartbreaks, giggling over cute boys. Sleepovers. Bike rides. All for one, and one for all. This is Life.

You know it when you're young, when your spirit is free.

Life......Is a celebration of you.

Single, Again
December 21

I had a premonition that something bad was about to happen three months before I found her letter. Never once had I reached my hand inside his briefcase. Never before had I picked up his phone. I trusted him, in some ways more than I trusted myself. He expected each of us to do the right thing at all times, so I had always believed he was doing the same. I climbed the stairs on autopilot. I walked into my room, and without thinking, bent over and pulled out the papers. They were the only thing in the bag I touched. I began to read.

It was like an out of body experience, holding it in my hand, reading her words. I walked out of my room and told my sons to go in their room and shut the door. He was two floors below, lying on the couch, watching sports. I opened the letter and began to read it to him, my words blowing a hole through his brain. All he wanted was possession of the papers, all I wanted was to rewind my life. I lost my mind and threw him out of the house.

The sound of his car starting, the garage door going down, his car pulling up the hill and away from the house, intensified my shock. I felt this numbness, and a weird sense of disbelief. After he left, my body and my mind went strangely calm. Did I want to scream? Why didn't I cry? Yes, I was protecting my two children, but there was something more.

We played as if nothing happened. It was the darkest night I have ever imagined. Not a star in the sky, no moon, no lights on outside or cars passing by. My son asked when his father was coming home? I froze. I wasn't ready for my family to fall apart. I had no plan for recovery, no plan for surviving the night. Like a robot I called. I expected the phone to ring and ring, imagined he had raced to her. He answered, and I told him the kids wanted him to come home. "Where are you?", I asked. In that moment, shock and fear consumed me. He wasn't far away, waiting in a ball park just down the road. Maybe he knew all along that I would call? I can't relive that dark evening without feeling the pain of 44-year-old me. Every time I tell it I am thrown back into that little boy's room.

Even then he had power over me. It felt like I was the naughty one, the one who had done something wrong. His power came from how easy he thought it would be to walk out the door.

When he called her the next day, she refused to leave her husband for him. Imagine the dynamics…his affair was controlled by her, and my marriage by him. He was wrapped around her finger and I was wrapped in his lies.

Single, Again
December 21

I walk slowly along my favorite beach on the southern coast of Maine, thinking about my life and how I will find peace. The waves keep count with my pain, and as I reach the turnaround, it starts to rain.

Some of the greatest lessons I have learned in my life took me to the breaking point in the most silent of ways. Not one person knew what was going on inside me, not even me. Hours in front of the mirror would never have told me what I needed to know. I face the ocean and say aloud, "Who am I?"

I slowly begin to walk back.

Single, Again
December 22

Dear 41-year-old me,

I have come to understand you in a way you cannot fathom right now. In a sense you have been split apart. Openly the world sees the "you" you think you owe them. One day you will realize that no one is really looking. No one is keeping track. All the people around you have their own stories to star in. Are you tuning into their show? Of course not.

Then there is your reality. The truth is that Single Girl never really thought about marriage and children. All of a sudden, she found herself in a life without a plan, and in love in a way she never imagined. Motherhood thrilled Single Girl. She wanted to prove to the world that she was worthy of this life. She deserved to be the woman she became when the love of her children transformed her. It would have been easy if he looked at her and believed. If he looked and saw love.

All the years of pretending blew up the day she found the letter. It was as if 41-year-old me were hit by a bus. But instead of an ambulance coming to take her away, the bus continued to drag her down the road.

Single, Again
December 25

I love when people that have been through hell walk out of the flames carrying buckets of water for those still consumed by the fire.

Stephanie Sparkles

Single, Again
December 26

Dear 41-year-old me,

I wish you knew how young and innocent you are. I wish, even more than that, so much more, that you knew how inherently lovely you are. I watch you hovered over the computer, committed to finding an answer to his behavior. The Why??? You're reading Marriage Builders.com and for a moment something makes sense. The bank account for love!! The concept that people's actions add to your personal account for them, until one day you find yourself in love.

How is it possible that all of the things you are doing for this man do not add up to love? And yet, "she" who is married to another has earned his love?

You formulate a hypothesis that he was never the "Most Important Person" in anyone's life. Until he met Her, and She made him believe that finally he was Superman. You stood before him and read her letter aloud, pacing back and forth while he stared at you in disbelief. Finally, you asked: "Are you all of these things?"

And now, I am watching you make excuses for a man whose behavior is selfish, self-centered, and self-absorbed. A breeze flows through your hair...that's me. I'm whispering gently in your ear, softly, so you'll feel my words in your heart....

"Someday, someone is going to really love you."

Single, Again
December 31.

Climbing into bed with another person's spouse is like driving away in someone else's car because you like it better.

Single, Again
January 1

The mirror will never tell you who you are.
Nor another.

If I hand you the power to judge me, I allow the world to decide what I should be.

If I look out instead of in, your words become my truth.

If silence becomes our language, and the ice begins to crack beneath your feet, stop.

Stop.

If you find yourself lost in the world you created, turn around.

Turn around.

Come back to me. I am always here. I am you.
You simply forgot to look.

Single, Again
January 2

The tip of the shovel slides easily through the dirt, and you pretend not to notice. You close your eyes to avoid the pain of the sound of the soil as it lands on the ground beside you. A cutting look, a snide remark, a disinterested wave, or is it disgust? Something you deserve for being something less than he desires?

Work harder.
Ask for nothing.
Perfect wife -Perfect home - Perfect children.
Work harder.
The only thing that changes, is you.

Single, Again
January 3

Dear 41-year-old me,

The shovel is working every day now, and you are surrounded in darkness. Your efforts to please him, and perfect you, are matching his pace. You make his favorite breakfast and place it beside his lunch. As he leaves, you pretend he isn't heading to her, but he is. They meet in the morning and celebrate their great fortune. They smile across the office, the secret glance that everyone sees, and no one can believe.

The garage door goes down and finally you can exhale. The anatomy of an affair, a relationship built around lies and deceit and fueled by the energy of secrecy.

You helped keep their secret. Your extensive research recommends: First become the perfect partner, then if he doesn't give her up, leave. Cut off all contact.

The garage door goes up and he is back. Dinner on the table, perfect house, perfect kids, broken wife.

It will get worse before it gets better. He looks at you and says, "Oh my God, look how old and miserable you look."

A pile of dirt lands at your feet.

Single, Again
January 3

I spent countless hours trying to figure out why my husband was having an affair. His father had cheated on his mother and they divorced at a time when divorce was rare. The impact of the divorce on his life was an open discussion. I was baffled by his mindless decision to follow in footsteps he knew would crush his three sons.

There were days the studying saved me. I didn't share my situation with many, and those who I did tell often believed his affair ended when I first found the letter. My discovery would never create the end, because I did not matter.

To you, about to cheat, I offer My Thoughts....
I beg you to....

1. Look at what you have, and rest assured you will ruin it.

2. Recognize that you are about to rob your children of a role model.

3. Accept that you can't have it all and you can't fix it once it's broken.

4. "Once a cheater, always a cheater" means that even if you only cheat once, you've lost the trust necessary to convince your spouse it will never happen again.

5. Before you act, stop and think about what is drawing you to this person. Are you running together? Does he

pay attention to you? Know what you are drawn to, go home, and have an honest conversation. Admit you are drawn to someone and why, and then give your spouse a chance to create that feeling at home.

6. No matter where you think your marriage is, Stop. Face what's missing and try to fix it.

7. If you can't fix it, leave. Leaving first is the best option for your family. Leave with your dignity and pride and the option to return.

8. No matter what excuses you are making in your head, no matter how sure you are that you won't get caught, or that this is "just sex" or, "your soul mate" or "I can't stop myself", you are wrong.

Relationships built on deceit do not last. You are showing another person what you are willing to do while in a committed relationship and she will never forget it. He knows you're a cheater, because you cheated with him.

Take a hard look at you before you roll the dice.

Single, Again
January 4

Dear you, gentle soul reading my words and understanding every thought,

I want to help you, so please listen carefully.

You are perfect, just the way you are. What do you deserve? You deserve kindness, acceptance, and love. Start by giving it to yourself. Whisper, "I love you." Whisper, "I am going to take care of you". Whisper, "You are going to be fine."

One day I looked in the mirror and thought, "Ugh, you look terrible." As I walked away, I thought again. I went back to the same mirror with the same face and sent a new message. "You are beautiful." And I looked it. I really looked beautiful. Every time you look in the mirror, tell yourself you're beautiful. Because you are.

They say that hind sight is 20/20, and there is no greater proof of that than when you look back at your life. I am using my vision to help both of us to heal. I turn back the pages of my life to Married Me. I am watching her shivering in the dark forest. I take her hand and lead her out. We don't belong there, where the thoughts make our heart race. The trees are not ours. It is a situation outside of our control, so we turn away from it and walk toward the sunshine.

The warmth of the yellow sun, a gentle breeze, and the whisper of "I love you" and suddenly our heartbeat is calm. Bring yourself to the warmth of the sun. Calm your heart.

Single, Again
January 6

25-year-old me wants to meet for coffee. It's December 27, 2017 and I have to work. She's insistent, so I go. The truth is, I'm excited to see her and hear what she has to say.

We meet at the Dunkins on Route 10 where the girl knows her order and has her coffee made before she opens the door. Nothing's changed. We get two.

25-year-old me, look at you, looking at me. What is it?? She reaches across the table and holds my hand. I feel her love flow through me. "It's time to let go. It's time to really love you."

I know she's right. "But what about all the things that have happened to me? The things I let happen? I need to protect us."

The look is long but soft. "We don't do that. We sing, we dance, we laugh, we love. The rest is baggage. What would be the worst thing that could happen?"

I reply, "What would be the best thing?"

She smiles. Come back to me....

Single, Again

January 7
2011

It's morning and I know in my head that I must get up, but the weight of my heart makes me weak. I get up several times and make it four steps, five steps, but each time I return to my bed. I don't want to be her, the one who can't get out of bed. I don't want to let the pain win.

The door opens, and my son crosses the room and climbs into my bed. I can't bear the thought that he sees me like this. His hand rubs my arm and he says, "Mom. Please." We both start to cry. He's 13 and deserves better than this. I say, "Here's what we are going to do. On the count of three we are getting up and making the bed, so no one can get in it." I turn the radio on and crank the volume.

It is in this moment that I discover the power of music.

Single, Again

January 8

Music is magical. It has the power to alter your moods and carry you away! The lyrics can make you believe you've just been through a break up, fallen in love, or lost a loved one. You hear the beat and your hips start to move, your foot tapping, a dance floor energized with boogie fever. It's the magic of filling your head with thoughts and watching your body respond. Music taught me something powerful.

You are the master of your mind. You can control your thoughts. You determine how you feel.

Years later I would discover that this powerful lesson has a name: Mindfulness.

Single, Again
January 11

What if you were given one bike, as a child, and this would be the only bike you would ever own. Would you leave it out in the rain?

And what if…you were given a baby, his care only to you? What would you feed him? What lullaby would you sing?

And what if…your heart, mind, and soul were your precious gifts? Only yours? And not replaceable….

2017
The Teacher

My shift was almost done when he walked into my department and stopped at the Creed counter. We began to talk, me spraying cards, him drifting over the bottles, pointing out the ones he already owns. He is tall and thin, and I like his look, but I love his vibe. His accent gives away that his was born in India, and he says, "I am here on business, but I come to Boston once every two months." I respond, "How long have you been living in New Jersey?" He begins to answer, but I start to laugh. "Wait. How did I know you were from New Jersey? Did you tell me that?" He smiles and asks if I have been meditating?

Meditating? I start to speak, and everything falls out at once. I want to tell him all of the things I have learned over the past few years, how I discovered the power of meditation, and how important it is to me now. We are short on time, so we cross over to Tom Ford and he says, "The next time you meditate try this. Breathe in the mantra: I am not my body. Breathe out: I am not my mind." He positioned his fingers over his nostrils so that the air would flow in one side and out the other. He explained how this would be beneficial to my brain. I promised myself to try this as soon as I get home.

We head back to Creed and I ask, "Do you know Dr. Brian Weiss?" He stops, and turns, and that's when I understand. My angel reader called it Living From Your Soul. She knows when she walks into a room, the people who are living a life of purpose. "Their eyes are brighter", she said.

I get ready to head home, my mind drifting over the words, 'you are not your mind, you are not your body.' In this moment, I am a student.

2017
Lessons

"I am not my mind." "I am not my body."

He told me to recognize that the mind is merely a place where memories are stored. The body, a vehicle to transport me on Earth, represents me, but is not me. Both are left behind when my time here is complete. Everything I have read and studied is in his beliefs, and I cannot wait to go home and try this meditation. I find peace in the words as they detach the anxiety of the world from my purpose here.

Never once in my marriage journey did I ask, "Why is this happening to me?" The journey of my life is to ask, "What is it that I am supposed to be learning from what is happening to me?" I am here for a purpose, to learn something very important to the part of me that I am.

I think about the concept of mind and body, and I recognize that they are pathways to my soul. I need to honor and care for these gifts. Every thought I have, every lesson presented before me, are all part of the reason I am here. Are they for my highest and best? When I take my body for a run, does my soul soar? My truth is that you cannot touch my hand without touching my heart without nurturing my soul.

I am my soul.

Single, Again
January 12

I believe I have loved her through many of my lives. We joke sometimes about that and she says, "How did you always know?" I have no answer from my head, only my heart. We have been there for each other through so many of our life struggles, without judgement or burden, only purpose.

She called to tell me she had been watching Oprah's Soul Sunday. "She has this man on, Dr. Brian Weiss, and everything he says is all of the things you believe." The next day, we meet for breakfast at our regular Dunkin. It was almost her birthday, and as usual, we had a lot to discuss.

"Hey, how about if for your birthday present, we go to Barnes and Nobles and I buy each of us one of his books?" We were planning our own mini book club and to switch books after. In the end we each kept our own books.

Dr. Weiss is a psychiatrist who discovered through hypnosis of a patient, that our souls travel through many lives. I found his book fascinating and very true to my belief that I am my soul.

I often think about the human struggle of sexuality and how many people feel trapped inside the body of a man, feeling like a woman. I believe that comes from a soul that has been many times one sex, and in this life a different one. I pray that we evolve to understand our life purpose, the growth of the soul, so that one day Blue and Pink will just be colors.

Single, Again
January 12

Dear 44-year-old me,

There will be many difficult days and nights to come. There will be stories filled with pain and confusion that may not fade as the years pass.

Will you ever truly understand? No, you will not.

Do you need to? No, you do not.

When you are 50 years old, you will have to come to peace with the reason why you stayed in a marriage that broke your soul. You know why you are doing it now, and some day you will be grateful you found the courage.

Here is your most honest truth:

The thought of going to bed at night without your babies was unthinkable. The idea that another woman might assume the role of "mother", and share Christmas morning, Easter, first day of everything and anything, with your children was unimaginable. Cracked was better than broken. So, you made a choice.

Nothing could hurt more than that. So, you stay. And you will never regret that choice.

Single, Again
January 13

Like a perfectly choreographed dance, Earth Angels drift swiftly into your life, just as you need them. As the music plays, pay attention to those who take your hand. Feel their love as they spin you across the floor. Know their strength as they carry you when the words blur, and the steps confuse. In this dance of life, you are never alone, you are never the only one.

And always remember, You, too, are an Earth Angel.

Single, Again

January 14

Dear 45-year-old me,

I wish I could rescue you from tonight.

Your sister and your mother drove from CT to watch your sons, so you can spend the night away. You look at the dress you bought and silently hope the salesperson was right. You looked him straight in the eyes, "This is a very important Event. I need to hide how skinny I am. Please." He chose the blue one. You could see from the look on your sister's face when you tried it on that she was worried about you. There was no hiding your 100-pound body behind glitter.

Together you drive to the hotel, small talk and fake smiles barely masking the stress of what is happening. He opens his computer and you take a shower and get ready. You wonder who he is typing to and what are they saying? He is calm and composed. You manage to get dressed, and drive to the Event. Together, you get on a shuttle filled with strangers dressed in sequins and expensive ties. Your whole body is shaking and the more you shake the angrier he gets at you. You want to stop, but you are in a full-blown panic attack. When the trolley stops, and you walk in, you will have to face her. You can hear your teeth chattering, your heart racing.

All of a sudden, a thought fills your body. Your blood goes warm and your heart calm. You know what you have to do, and the words fill your mind.

"I forgive you."

Single, Again
January 15

2017

Today

I could never have imagined the life I am living today.

I could never have anticipated the happiness, the kind that feels like bubbles are coming out of you when you laugh…drifting up toward the stars and popping… just in time to sprinkle joy on your face. No one could have prepared me for the tickle of his touch. The trust. The honesty. The raw and undeniable thrill of two people lying on a beach, staring at the sky, just as the shooting star you were seeking dances across the sky. We are laughing and screaming at the same time. "OH MY GOD!!! DID YOU SEE THAT?!?!" And then I am hugging him and he's laughing. And it's pure magic.

I never would have believed I would feel all of this. Because for the longest time I felt nothing at all.

Single, Again

January 16

It's been a year and still the scent of presidential drama permeates the fabric of our lives. It brought out the worst in many of us, and I believe we will look back on this time in horror that we lost friends over a man we will never meet. But that's for another blog. What I want to talk about is the slogan that lit this nation on fire:

MAKE AMERICA GREAT AGAIN.

The first time I read that, I stopped dead in my tracks. America, by definition, is We. We the people. It is our actions that bring about change. All eyes are on One Man to make us great, but where does great begin?

Great begins in the home. The most important job I will ever have is as a mother. Our greatness relies on the strength of our smallest unit. Here we learn our values and here we learn to love.

I drew a mental circle around my world to include the things I feel responsible for, and I can control. My heart, my children, my home, my community, and my job. Who am I in this world? Like a teacher in a classroom, the leader is only as successful as the student's behavior. How can He make America Great Again if "we" don't participate? If some of the followers are made to feel ashamed?

There's a lot of talk about who belongs here. To the minorities I would say "minority" means "fewer" not "less than." Be proud of your heritage, the color of your skin, the shape of your eyes, your religion. Don't wait for acceptance, embrace who you are, and get busy helping to make America great.

Maybe when things crack, they grow back together stronger than before? Like me.

Single, Again
January 17

2014

My cell phone rang just as I passed through the Cambridge toll. I answered, "Are you calling to tell me you're moving to Boston?"

The voice from Wisconsin gasped, "How did you know?"

Because I needed her. And just like that, my Earth Angel arrived.

Single, Again
January 18

He's in 3rd grade and I can see he's upset. "A kid at school said I'm a %#+*". I look at him wide eyed and say, "Did it work??!?" He gives me the curious look and I say, "Ok, let's try this again. Ready?" I stand in front of him and say, "Poof!!! You're a rock!!" Nothing happens. "Poof! You're a tree!" Again…nothing. "Hmmmm…I guess calling you something doesn't make it true."

Sometimes, even when we know something is not true, we are still affected by the messages that come our way. It's important to be careful who you let near your ears.

Sometimes you have to pull the bus over and let people off. And drive away.

Single, Again
January 20

The branch is steady and strong, and the little bird walks slowly to the end, looking out at the beautiful world that surrounds her. She's been given new wings, and she looks at them in awe. In a few moments she is going to take a deep breath and leave the branch.

It isn't what we see coming that breaks our wings. It's what hits us from behind and makes us lose the faith that what we see is what is.

Jump, little bird...

Single, Again
January 21

There was a night, not worthy of discussion, that brought me to my knees. All of his belongings, in bags at the curb. A car racing down the driveway, a hotel room, a plea for coffee the next day. I would sit and watch his lips move.

"You are not the right kind of man for me." Even as I spoke, I knew I would let him back. Again, the lips move, and words come out.

"I will make you want me to never leave. And if the day comes that you cannot get over what I have done, it will be a very short conversation."

This would be his greatest lie.

Single, Again

January 22

"There's going to come a day when you are going to have to decide what makes you happy. And when you do, you can't be thinking about me and my brothers."

I turn and smile, but what I am thinking is...how does he know?

Single, Again
January 23

The grass is so green and the sky so far away. I can feel the Earth moving beneath me and with it my thoughts. Why am I here? My wonders drift through the mystery of technology and the amazing miracle of modern language. There must be a greater purpose to my existence. I feel rooted to Earth and yet pulled toward the stars.

I am 15 and I absolutely love being alive.

Single, Again
January 24

I am 51 and travel back to lay on the grass beside 15-year-old me. She can't see me, she doesn't know I am here, or that we will eventually be blonde. I remember these summer evenings with such clarity. I would spend an hour running across the yard as fast as I could and end in some kind of flip that made me feel like I was flying. I am a swimmer, a runner, and in this moment, a gymnast.

I want so badly to tell her the secrets that will come in time. I bring my lips to her ear and I begin....

"Your purpose in life is to love. You will love through pain, through confusion, and through doubt. You will love to tears, the first grader on the stage singing in a holiday chorus, the boy on the mound, the young man crossing the stage with a diploma. You will love people you meet once, or many times, from places you live, and countries you will never see. You will grow to value only love.... not material items that can slip through your fingers, or a face that that will wrinkle and a body that will age.

And one day, you will look in the mirror and realize the greatest challenge of your life. You must love you."

2015

Part of digging yourself out of the Dark Hole is remembering who you are.

Single, Again
January 26

The State Open finals 1983. 100 butterfly steps up to the blocks, and there is a lane empty. I touch my coach's arm, say his name. Time stands still as he stops the meet just before the gun goes off. The swimmers step down, the lanes are readjusted, and I walk in disbelief away from my team.

I was the alternate, and now the lane belongs to me.

Single, Again
January 27

Dear 43-year-old me,

One day you will look back and see that today begins your road to recovery. You saw your boss talking to your work husband and you felt hurt. When she walked away, he said, "Oh yea, we are getting a new line in Saks and she wants to know if you want to work here?"

Life is funny.

She approached you the next day and you thanked her for the offer and declined. He didn't want you to take the job. He thought it was too many hours, too much time away from home. She said, "Ok, I'll put you down for a 2:00 interview" and walked away.

Life has a plan.

Trust it,
Me

Single, Again
January 29

It's raining and cold, and the last thing I want to do is open my window to get the mail. I flip the box open, grab the small pile, drop it on my lap, and quickly close the window. As I am about to turn down my driveway, I see the familiar writing.... of 25-year-old me.

I can't wait to hear what she says.

Single, Again
January 30
2009
The Interview

I am standing outside the door listening to a woman speak on the phone. She doesn't know I'm here waiting to interview. I am angry because I don't know why I am here. There is no way I am accepting this job, and I am furious with myself for even standing here waiting to deal with this conversation. And suddenly the door opens, to the office, to my life.

We sit down at a table with the most beautiful bottles I have ever seen. She is the kind of woman every woman wants to be, and I really like her. We have the kind of conversation two people have when one has nothing to lose. She looks at me and tells me she wants to put all of her cards on the table. "What do I have to do to get you?"

Opportunity changes our path. Married girl is about to learn who she is in a world defined by her.

I accepted the job.

2018
I am boarding a plane to Dallas with one goal in mind, to work on this book. I am assigned a center seat toward the back of the plane and as I walk down the aisle my eyes are met by an adorable woman. She has the window seat and smiles as I climb over the woman and get settled. I grab my phone and get to work on my post as she calls her father to let him know she is safely

on the plane. As the plane takes off, she begins to ask me questions about myself. Initially, I am awkward and nervous, and my ears are popping so my voice sounds weird. I tell her I am writing a book and she responds, "About divorce, I hope."

We spend the next 4 hours talking nonstop about her life and mine. I don't believe in accidental meetings and I realize I am looking at myself from a different time. She is at a crossroad that I faced 10 years ago, and this meeting really made me think about the importance of rebuilding yourself after a divorce from a career perspective. When I was married and in crises, I turned to work. I believe work is the single most effective way to have a positive impact on your self-esteem. Working hard helped me rebuild me. Often times for women, we have put our career on hold to raise a family, and suddenly we have to begin again. After 20 years, my college degree did not translate to a career. To leave my marriage I needed to be able to support myself, full time, with health insurance. For many women, this is a heavy burden. I asked her, "What is your plan?"

Every woman needs a plan. The first step is to get out of bed and say, "Get out of my way." She said, "Ok, who am I saying that to? Myself?" I said, "Yes, anyone that is in your way needs to get out of your way. It is time for you to find out what you are made of. You have children watching everything you do." Fear cannot get in your way. You cannot wait for a man to rescue you, not the one from your past nor the one in your future. Not getting your S&%^ together is the one thing you cannot afford to do.

Single, Again
February 1

For more than one year I didn't look up unless I was forced to. My new job gave me a place to get lost in, and I went at it as if my life were held in the balance. My greatest truth is that I had stopped feeling, even the nervousness that fed me for years was gone. Like a train speeding through the night, I just wanted to survive the miles without anything touching me.

It worked for a while. The walls I built were tall and strong and I was bullet proof. Luckily for me, I didn't see the cracks forming. I didn't see the skinny blonde climbing the wall with her free spirit and craving for fun. She took one look at me and had another plan.

Friends are like that.

Single, Again
February 2

Yesterday, 2017

Love

We're walking back from the beach. It's raining, and we don't know we've been out here for three hours, talking and laughing, saying the same thing at the same time. We're climbing rocks and porch steps to a house we dream to own and pretend we do. He takes my hand when he thinks it's dangerous and I like that. He watches me do things I would only do in front of him because being me when I am with him comes easily. He points out my dream house in the distance and I start yelling "Oh my god!!! The house is right there!?!?!" I start jumping up and down, with my hands holding my head in disbelief!! I'm almost crying when I ask if we can walk to the house, and when I turn to him, he is smiling. He doesn't think I'm weird. He gets me, the real, true, exposed me.

We are walking home, and I ask, "Why is this so easy?" And he says, "Because neither of us wants power over the other."

My next breath, I am certain, is helium.

Single, Again
February 4

Our greatest obligation in life is to be true to ourselves. In this truth is the knowledge of who we are, the need for pure and true love, and our voice. It entitles us to seek our dreams and live with passion. It uncovers our happiest, most successful, most dignified version of our self. To be true to yourself is the highest form of self-love...where our thoughts, words, and actions line up with our souls.

Life is meant to be lived from the inside out, not the other way around. First you need to love who you are and then give that to the world. I lived backwards.... deciding first what the outside world expected of me and then molding me to that. It's the dream that I could be perfect. Seeking perfection, living through the eyes of others, denying that you and your happiness matter, is what happens in a relationship like married girl had. I know the loneliness, pain, and shame of that life.

Once I was honest about who I am and what I was feeling, I discovered something very different than an argument from "the outside world."
I discovered Love.

Single, Again
February 6

Truth

I used to wonder how many munchkins would equal one donut? One day I decided 6. Today I noticed the calorie content is posted on each item and now I know the truth.

At the end of your life you will have all the answers, and when you do, will you wish you ate the 6th donut anyway?

Single, Again
February 8

The sun comes up, and a beautifully wrapped package floats through your window and lands on the carpet next to your bed. Your heart flutters at the sight of its mesmerizing sparkle, and you must touch it. The covers thrown back, toes on the floor, you reach for it. Just as your fingertips meet the brightly colored paper...it floats just a bit from you. You reach again, and it floats just outside your reach. The scent is divine, and you can feel the possibilities of what's inside...if you can just capture it. With both hands you reach up...as it drifts above you...on your toes...you've almost got it....

Time.

Single, Again
February 9

Time. We think we control it. We believe that it comes to us in an abundance so great that we can wait to live until "later".

I sat in a truck stop at Dunkin and watched his lips move, hearing nothing, but planning in my head when I would leave. End the pain. Finally know when the ambulance would come, pick me up and let me heal.

In the fog of my thoughts I decided on next September when my second child left for college. I could make it until then. I would pass through the tunnel of time with my eyes closed and my breath held.

Little did I know, in another home in the same town, a family I adored would measure time quite differently. Time would be treasured by the number of moments they could hold their father's hand, listen to his voice, his laugh, feel his love. Time would be controlled by cancer, and it would be a precious gift.

Single, Again
February 11

There were days when I opened my mouth to speak, and as I listened to my own words, I realized I was hearing them for the first time.

Single, Again
February 12

I trip over myself trying to get into the house to read the letter from 25-year-old me. It's been 26 years since I have seen her writing and heard her voice. My hands are shaking as I unfold the paper and begin...

"If you are reading this letter, you have already found me."

The letter drops from my hands.

Single, Again
February 13

I found her? When? What were we doing? Why wasn't it more obvious to me? I imagine myself running down a beach and crashing into her arms. Bustling through the city and turning on just the right corner at just the right moment. I imagine myself falling asleep one night and finding her in a dream. If I found her, where did she go?

I believed I would go back to find her and suddenly be healed. Whole. Unbreakable. Healing doesn't happen all at once. Sometimes I declare myself Healed, only to find myself better the next day. And there are times when something happens that opens my wounds. Suddenly I am raw and vulnerable all over again.

I whisper to myself, "Will I ever really heal?"

I pick the letter back up and begin to read, knowing the real challenge has been staying out of the Dark Forest.

Single, Again
February 14

I pick the snow globe up off the table and give it a good shake. The once calm and peaceful world is filled with tiny white snowflakes. One shake, a storm. Eventually the flakes will float back, and no one will see them or know they were there.

At the base of the globe, a woman sits in a tiny plastic house built for her. She cannot leave the house and sweep up the flakes. The snow and the globe are not hers to control, nor does she want to. The woman in the plastic house in the plastic village in the tiny globe has gained wisdom.

She knows peace comes from within. It never mattered how many times the globe was shaken; the key was how she reacted to the storm.

Single, Again
February 16

She rolls over and moans, her sheets soaked from the fever that broke during a fitful sleep. Every muscle in her body aches, her throat raw with infection, her head pounding. What time is it? What day? Her body is so weak she cannot imagine standing or walking across the room. A sliver of light along the door frame, the shuffling of feet, the outline of a body beside her bed. The clinking of ice against the glass, a straw pressed to her lips, a soft voice whispering, "Drink"…

How many glasses of water have been given to her in her lifetime? Without significance?

This time was different, she was different, and she knew: This one meant everything.

Gratitude

I have learned some of the greatest lessons of my life when I was in the darkest place imaginable. I believe that we learn the deepest meaning of something when we are without it. Imagine being lost in a cave, for a week, terrified you will never get out. You have no food, no water, no companionship. The only sound you hear is your footsteps on the gravel. Suddenly, you feel a hand on your arm, guiding you out of the cave. Will water ever feel the same against your lips? Will you ever take for granted the taste of your breakfast? The warmth of a hug?

When what you lived without comes back to you, you suddenly become acutely aware of what it is. When love is lost, and then it's found, it means everything.

Single, Again
February 17

It turns out the skinny blonde was a package deal. One blonde, she was soulful, clairvoyant, and sensitive. She was like finding Home. I was drawn to her ups and downs, her stories, her laugh, her nuttiness. And the skinny blonde, on a tirade to put her life back together as quickly as f'n possible. She was running her own legal circus, passionate, determined and fearless. Skinny Blonde was like finding a jet plane at my front door with Shania Twain blasting "Let's Go Girls" out the window.

At first, I watched them from a distance, with just one eye, the way you drive past a dead animal in the road. They wore pearls and bright lipstick and had the sparkle of an infectious giggle. I stepped closer, day by day, realizing as I walked that I had forgotten how it felt to have a friend and be a friend. The joy of being a girl was lost under the layers of secrecy and shame. From where I stood, it looked sooooo good.

I took a deep breath and jumped.

Single, Again
February 18

2014

The church was filled to capacity and I was sitting about ten rows from the front on the right-hand side of the aisle. I could see the back of his children's heads and his wife, my friend, the love of his life. I could not fathom what this day was like for them. I started to cry from the depth of my soul and I was fighting to keep my pain quiet. Up ahead to the right, seated alone, was his best friend from childhood, his best friend today. We had only met weeks before, brought together by cancer and the love of this family. I looked down at my feet, praying to keep my sob private, when all of a sudden, I think…. "He is here." My blood goes warm and my body calms.

He would give a beautiful eulogy, we would go to the cemetery in the days ahead and plant flowers, and he would change the path of my life. I would tell him everything about my life and he would teach me about my compass and how to follow it. He was the hand that reached down into the dark hole and pulled me up. We would walk together for a period of my life and then his path would go one way and mine another.

Like a perfectly orchestrated dance, people come in to your life exactly when you need them. I believe life is a journey riddled with lessons on a path sprinkled with angels. Imprinted in my heart and my mind are all of my personal angels.

Gratitude.

Single, Again
February 19

Dear 45-year-old me,

I relive this day over and over in my mind and each time it gets dearer to me. It's like seeing the sun in the sky and then discovering the sunset, the day you met Them. It was a typical Sunday at Saks when the door whisked opened, and a red carpet rolled from the door to where I stood. In the background, Barbara Streisand was singing, and doves were flying above their heads. As our eyes met, a fantastic fireworks display went off. As the lights exploded, tiny bits of Gucci colored sparkle landed on the floor around us. And in my hair.

This was the day I met My Queens.

Standing there in awe, you don't realize yet how important these two will be for you. You don't know about the tall blonde they will bring you, or the strong little brunette, or the friends and family that will become yours. Their love and admiration will make you strong. But for the moment, just stand there and watch them sparkle.

Love,
Me
Gratitude

Single, Again
February 20

I keep thinking, "There's gonna come a day…". I might be walking out to my garage and the thought pops into my head, like it did just now, as it will again tomorrow, until I can finish the sentence. For the moment, I don't want to finish the thought. I want it to linger in my mind and mean a million things. It means Possibilities. Opportunities. It stands for change, empowerment, and goals. It signifies that "what is" is ever changing, and that what lies before me is new and exciting and Mine.

There's gonna come a day…….

Single, Again
February 22

2015

Most of what we did was structured and in patterns. Every Saturday and Sunday we got up and went to the gym, ran with a friend, stopped for a coffee, and drove home. I would look out the window and wonder why I had grown to hate this so much. And then one Sunday, something changed...he left while I was getting dressed.

I decided I had two options. Option 1 was stay mad and stay home. Option 2 was to get in my car and go. I went with Option 2, and drove, heart pounding, to the gym.

When he saw me, he pretended to think I wasn't coming. We both knew why he left. My reply to him never really mattered. He said, "Why does it always have to be about you?"

"Well, it is Mother's Day."

Single, Again
February 23

Dear 26-year-old me,

I am chasing you down the aisle of the church to tell you something. I reach you just as your father lifts the veil over your face and kisses you gently on the cheek. You lean in and hug him. A hug that means "I'm going to be ok". A hug that means, "I'll always be here for you." Before you turn to face the groom, I take your hand and bring it to my lips. My free hand drifts over your belly and our eyes meet. You are meant to bring this boy into the world, to be his mother, love him, guide him.

Pure love, faith, and the dream of a beautiful family brought you to this moment in time. And as I stand here now, with your hand to my lips, I promise you I would do it all again. Over and over and over....

Love,

Me....single again

Single, Again
February 24

It's the end of my life and I am standing before the brightest lights I have ever seen, a cylinder of vivid colored lights streams from the ceiling to the floor. Everything that has ever happened to me, every thought, every feeling, floods back through my mind, playing the movie of me. And I see what I knew all along, every time I closed my eyes and said, "Please, just show me who you are so I can thank you." The pennies that were everywhere, the numbers on the clock, all the times I opened my mouth to speak and they were your words I heard. Words I needed to hear.

I just wanted to see who you were and now I hear myself gasp, "Oh my God, you're here!!!" I walk to the circular stream of colored lights flooding from my ceiling. As I wrap my arms around it, it flows inside me. I am flooded with the greatest love I have ever known.

And then I wake up.

Single, Again
February 25

In his mind I have become the daydreamer. He catches me staring, lost in thought, heavy under a blanket of emotions. He smiles when he says it, like it's a cute joke we share between us. The truth is that I've grown weary. I'm tired of the pretending, tired of accepting a life I didn't bargain for. I drift into thought again. Why do people keep telling me I am so strong? Is there strength in denial? Strength in acceptance? I want to be so weak, so incredibly weak that no one would dare hurt me. How long have I been this "strong" woman? My whole life? Or have I morphed into her, silently over time, in the way that the outside becomes firm and resilient while the inside melts? Or because the inside is melting?

I see my reflection in the rear-view mirror, and I ask the sad eyes I see…. "Which way are we going?"

Single, Again
February 27

Married girl sits up and turns to the groom. He has no idea this is coming, and neither does she. "I am not divorcing you, but I have to move downstairs and think. All I can hear is your voice in my head and I need to hear my own thoughts."

She grabs a pillow and every ounce of courage and walks out of the room. In the hallway is her youngest boy. He looks at her with his big brown eyes and says, "I'm coming too."

And down the stairs they went.

Single, Again
February 28

The glow of the sun illuminates the landscape of the hill ahead in vibrant pink and yellow, signifying the start of a new day. Married girl walks along the path that has become familiar to her married life. She can feel the small pebbles lost in the dirt as they press into the soles of her feet, reminding her that she has taken her shoes off and thrown them into the brush. The grass is dewy, and the air is fresh. Married girl takes a deep breath and stares at the fork in her road.

Choices

Single, Again
March 2

Married girl turns around and looks down the path behind her. Her eyes follow the imprint of her feet back from where she came. There is pain in her heart, pain from the gratitude she feels for the life she has lived. In the footprints are all the memories of the children, their little hands in hers, an infant's head nestled in an elbow, a fever at night. She hears footsteps running down the stairs, the sound of feet heading to school, or a game, or to Christmas morning?

All those years she lived with the fear of a family lost. She knows now that there were five of us, and four stayed on the path. The family 26-year-old me dreamed of survived. Every bit of what she sees was real. It was outside where the world blurred. The chaos was a man.

Married girl turns back around and faces the choices of her future. She tightens the straps of her backpack and turns right.

Single, Again
March 3

We climb down the two flights of stairs to our guest room where two queen beds await our arrival. I take the one on the left and he starts to arrange all of his things on the right. He's been like this his whole life. He brings every single thing with him from one bed to another, and I love watching him. We settle under our covers and start to whisper. I wonder what this night would have felt like if he didn't follow me? Would I have been scared? Given in and gone back upstairs? The truth is that my boy needed me just as much as I needed him in that moment. I had gotten lost in my head and let him drift just a little too far. Lying there I felt it.

This was the first night in my journey out of my marriage. It would not be "a short conversation" and he would not "understand and leave." Upstairs was a man who was discovering for the first time what it feels like to fear the loss of his family.

Single, Again
March 4

2017
Yesterday

I am at work. It's the kind of day that starts with an awards ceremony that empowers, incites laughter and pride in even the smallest success. Suddenly one woman claims, "We are family!!" and another "I'm like Meryl Streep at the Grammys!!" I look around me, at all of the women who have a story outside of the one we share, and I am grateful that I am part of this one. I am grateful.

We scatter as the store opens and I hear Meryl Streep telling one of her stories and I want to run full speed to her and hug, hug, hug her. Her words are saturated in honesty and openness and I want to BE that. Not ashamed and secretive and private and scared. I open the windows of my heart and armful by armful, I empty the closets of my soul until all that is left is the sweet smell of gratitude.

I want to own my story. The good, the bad, and the ugly. I want to be me and know I'm ok.

Single, Again
March 5

> In order to become something,
> I have to first See it.
> In order to See it,
> I have to first Want it.
> In order to want it,
> I have to first Believe.

The Anatomy of Change

Single, Again
March 6

Night one

I rolled over onto my left side to face where my young son was sleeping. His slow, deep, rhythmic breath lulled me into relaxation. I could feel my body unwind, and I wondered how long have I been this tense? When did I start holding my breath? This wasn't the first time I had slept alone. There were business trips for him, and nights of severe insomnia when I slipped away to a couch. This was different. The tide inside me had changed.

The voice that told me I could never live without him, the one that silenced Single Girl, couldn't hear the messages that came from a world he never entered. He couldn't hear the words that came in my left ear and pushed his out the right. He couldn't see the effects of a job successfully done, that he demanded I quit because it was ruining our marriage. He didn't know I had friends, that I found a happy place, that I saw a light. This was different.

The Anatomy of Change

Single, Again
March 7

2017
Tonight....

We are in my kitchen, eating carrots and humus, drinking wine. Casual conversation, but I notice everything about him. How blue his eyes look, the perfect haircut, how he laughs while he talks, and then he tells me a story about his son. And I am suddenly crying…because in his story he is everything I have ever dreamed of.

He says, "What?"

"You are such a good man." My heart explodes. "I am so lucky."

Love

Single, Again
March 8

The next few months would be the most difficult to look back on. There were nights that I would grab my youngest and flee to my Angel from Wisconsin's house. My whole body would be shaking as I called and asked, "Can we come?" I would arrive to open arms, and I would talk, and she would listen. Eventually I would have to let her sleep. For the next several hours I would lie in her guest bed not knowing how I would face the day that was creeping closer and closer.

When the tables turned, and he felt his life slipping away from him, he sought control in the angriest of ways. The first Christmas after we separated was the worst time in our married life. He spun out of control, and that was bad, but that wasn't the worst part. What I can't, even now, explain...

Is that I went back.

Single, Again
March 9

It's two days before Christmas and she can't believe she's calling me and telling me to sleep at her house. She knows he has my phone and is on a rampage, yelling at her son and mine, and threatening "the hand that reached down into the dark hole to pull me up." This is the first Christmas since her husband has died and the last thing, she needs is this. She insists.

I plan to go there directly from work, but as I drive down the highway, I change my mind. How dare he threaten me? I drive home and pull into the driveway, relieved that there are no other cars home. As I enter the home, I hear the shower running and I am relieved. I climb the stairs and I can hear him singing Christmas carols, which shocks me after the day we have had. I grab a bag and start stuffing clothes for work and sleeping into the bag. I search everywhere for my phone, but it is not there. I decide to take his phone and iPad hostage while I use a hanger to unlock the bathroom door. There, between the two sinks, is my phone. I slam his down and pick mine up as he tears the shower curtain open. His eyes are in rage. I glare right back and say, "Trade ya." I drop his iPad on the carpet and begin to leave. As I run down the stairs, he hurls insults at me, and I think...what happened to the short conversation?

Everyone in her house is trying to pretend that life is in some way normal. But it's not, because we are all, for our own reasons, in shock. She and I climb into her bed and start to talk, first about me, but then it's her turn. She says, "I am so incredibly sad." I get up from the bed and I go to the closet where all of his clothes hang, and I take a shirt and bring it back to the bed. I tell her, "Please, hug it and try to smell him." She takes the shirt in her arms and buries her face in it, the loss falling out of her in tears. In the darkness I can see everything clearly. We are two women with the same name...

And we are the greatest story of irony ever written.

Single, Again
March 12

You get so used to the pattern of things, so comfortable with your role...mother, sister, daughter, friend...that you get weaved into your existence in a way that traps you. You lose sight of the fact that there was a time when 'Who you are to others' was chosen by you. You chose to be his wife. You vowed 'til death do you part. You vowed for better or for worse.

It seemed at the time like a perfect plan. You believed the role was made for you because the vision you had, came from a place of truth within you. Until your truth was no longer The Truth.

How do you now cut yourself loose? There are people who have come to count on You being You. How can you turn to them and say, "That isn't me. I am not her anymore?"

And what do you do when after all this, you let him come home?

Single, Again
March 12

In February I went to my mother's house so that
he could pack his things and move out.

Single, Again
March 13

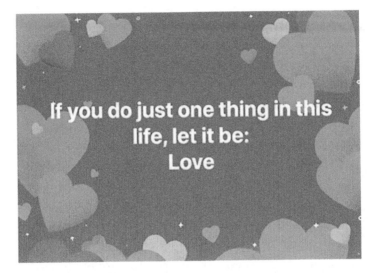

Single, Again
March 13

Together you choose mediation not because it's better but because it's cheaper. Neither of you has any idea what you are doing. Divorce is new and riddled with pain. Even though you want it and know it's the best choice for you, you know nothing at all. You walk into the mediator's office on autopilot and he is cockier than ever. He keeps getting up from his chair to help himself to the candy bowl, tossing it into his mouth like this is a game and he has nothing to lose. You are nervous, and your voice cracks and you cry. Of course, you cry. You are talking about custody, holidays, and when the children are no longer children. Your head is spinning, wondering how it will feel to live out this plan?

It's over and you walk out, going down the stairwell instead of the elevator. He's behind you asking why you are crying? He says, "We don't have to do this." You want to turn to him and yell, WE didn't do this! But it seems too obvious and would take energy you don't have. You're outside and walking to your car and it seems absurd that the sun is out. It's June and you are going to renew your license from here, because yours is expiring at the same time your marriage is. He asks for a ride to his house because you have his golf clubs in your car. You agree, not thinking, because autopilot has kicked in and you can't think. This moment will never seem normal again, but it is part of the lesson. As you're driving into his parking lot, he smiles and asks, "Wanna come up and see the place?" You say, "No." Are you kidding me right now? Just take your clubs and leave. "Come on up, you should see where the boy you love so much sometimes sleeps when he isn't with you."

The door is opening, and you know this is a bad idea. If only you would listen to yourself…just once. We climb the stairs of a big old home where lost and broken people move when it's the only choice they have. That's how it looks and that's how it feels. He opens the door and you go in. There are pieces of your home moved here, and in that moment the sight of it is too much for you. You are crying so hard now that you need the wall to hold you up. You are leaning into the wall with both your arms crossed in front of your forehead. He says, "I knew this would upset you, but I didn't think this much." He is perfectly calm.

You talk for an hour, or he talks, and you listen, and everything he says is everything he never did before. Promises. A future that would be exactly what you agreed upon the day long ago when you walked down the aisle of a church. You stand up to leave. He says, "Please, let's go have lunch." You turn, and he is sitting in a chair you bought together many years before as a gift for him. You walk to where he is and sit down on his lap. You kiss him. Every ounce of pain you have felt over the past 7 years was in that kiss.

And then you leave.

Single, Again
March 14

Divorce is the un-weave.

It's the dismantle.

It's the erase of the story written in permanent marker.

It's the most familiar things becoming extraordinarily bare.

You know you knew him, but you can't remember him.

Divorce is the path splitting in two, with one foot on each path.

And then two feet on one path.

Single, Again
March 14

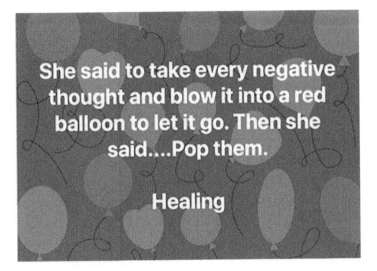

She said to take every negative thought and blow it into a red balloon to let it go. Then she said....Pop them.

Healing

Single, Again
March 15

She is deep in sleep, lost in a dream, when the alarm goes off. Eyes still closed she searches for her phone, her hand stumbling over the contents of the bedside table until it feels the familiar thin metal of her phone. Why does morning come so quickly? Why is the bed so cozy and the air so cold? She wants to stay wrapped up in the safety of the blanket, but life is on the other side of its warmth.

She wakes the boy for school and methodically dresses herself for the ritual. Ties her sneakers and heads to the car with the boy she adores. They do just about the same thing every day, because it makes sense, because it's what they have to do. Because it's what's expected.

The school sits on the perfect running route for her, a sidewalk on a winding road that leads to the center of town. It's a road lined with houses built at a time when life seemed easier. She parks her car in the school lower parking lot where parents park for concerts, meetings, and soccer games. The keys are dropped behind a tire, earbuds placed in her ears, a quick stretch, and she begins.

She begins....

Single, Again
March 16

Dear 47-year-old me,

You are going to look back and wonder, and here is what you will discover…

You have always been exactly where you belonged. There was no mistake, no moment when you should have gone left but went right. Your journey is as it was meant to be, and you will know it in your heart. Let your mind look, let it question, let it doubt, and then let your heart lead you back.

This is how I know….

The day you walked down the aisle, you did it for love. You entered into a marriage because you meant to, because you wanted to, and because you loved him. And that is how it should be.

Every day that followed you were driven by love. The love of children, the love of home, the love of commitment, the love of life. This is how it should be. And it is how it was.

When you look back, I want you to know that love spread like a wildfire everywhere you looked. You could not control the world, you could only ever control yourself…the choices you made, the way you lived, what you gave of yourself to the world around you, and how you respected the gift of love that came back.

And when you look to the moment it all changed, I want you to be grateful. Grateful that what happened around you did not make you into someone you did not want to be.

One day you are going to be me, and you are going to see that everything that happened along the way happened for a reason. They were lessons. They tested what you were made of. And in the end, you will know without a doubt:

You are made of love.

Hugs,
Me

Single, Again
March 18

It's February and 49-year-old me opens her eyes to a sun-drenched bedroom. The sense of peace that fills her body is exciting, exhilarating, joyful. She takes the time to soak it in and appreciate what today is: The first day she is alone in her home.

There will be many mornings after this when the sun would burst into her room making her feel thrilled to be alive, but never like this Single Day. His voice had found its way deep into her soul, shaking her confidence and crushing her self-esteem. All the times she curled in a ball on her bathroom floor sobbing were over. Never again would she hear, "How would you ever live without me?" His voice would fade over time, and her heart would heal. And love would come and sweep her off her feet. Today the sun lit her world. Today was the beginning, today…

She is Single, again.

Single, Again
March 19

For Married Girl, Single, Again was not a destination she could have prepared herself for. It's an eyes-closed-pray the parachute goes off-leap. It's a soft landing somewhere, anywhere with just one instruction: Get back up.

Imagine running through a dark maze in search of a door you aren't sure is there, and then seeing the light at the bottom of the door and bursting it open.

That's Single, again.

What's on other side of the door never crossed her mind.

Single, Again
March 20

The Chicago Marathon would be by far my favorite. The city gathers at every inch with music and cheering and the course is set up so that you are always turning corners on fairly flat roads. It was a blast and I qualified for Boston by one second. Imagine that!

In December, I began my training and for the first time in my life I was exhausted. And then I went to wash my hands and discovered one very red, very swollen joint. My heart skipped a beat. I called my doctor, and on a very snowy day when I was out battling to shovel my driveway, my diagnosis was confirmed. Rheumatoid Arthritis.

I scoured the internet in search of a cure. There wasn't a book that I didn't read, a theory I didn't consider. The typical drug path was worse than the disease itself. I put $20 in my pocket and ran the marathon.

The extent to which this disease would take from my life was up to me.

Single, Again
March 22

"The hand that reached down to pull me up" quickly became my BFF. I felt a pull to him I didn't recognize. It was as if an energy-filled wire connected us and was pulling me to him. He was easy to talk to. I trusted him as he gently lifted me from the dark place and placed me on the ground. I needed so badly what he offered so easily, a friend who made me believe I was lovable.

He called one night and asked if I was free Friday night? There was an extra ticket to see Taylor Swift with his sister and his daughters. My friend would also be there, the one who lost her husband, with her daughter. Could I go? I couldn't believe it!

The night was misty, but we didn't care. We ate dinner and walked in the rain to the stadium. I was excited to be out and in the company of these amazing women. Inside I was giggling, a pinch me moment that felt in a way like a dream come true. I sat in my seat, taking it all in, the lights of the stadium twinkling around me. I kept thinking, "I can't believe he did this for me."

Taylor's voice filled the stadium. Everything about her is surreal. Her clothes, her hair, her height…she's a larger than life doll. Suddenly, Ed Sheeran came on stage and they're singing 'Everything Has Changed.' I had been living in such a bubble that I didn't even know who he was. But I knew it was a magical moment.

I turn to my BFF's daughter and say, "I can't believe I have to go to the bathroom!" I'm running up the cement stairs when all of a sudden, I hear a song start and I can't leave. I turn around and for a moment, it's just me and Taylor and I am sooo sure she's singing to me. I know with every fiber of my being that I will never forget this moment. Not the sound, the lights, or the way the song enters my soul and takes over my being.

It's just me and Taylor and we are singing at the top of our lungs, with every ounce of girl power we have:

"We!! Are Never! Ever! Ever! Ever! getting back together!!"

And just like that, the greatest fireworks show of all time goes off behind the stage, celebrating me and Taylor, and every Single Girl in the world.

Single, Again
March 24

You have this idea, this definition of Being Single that comes from growing up. It's hanging out with your friends, going out to a bar with a couple of girls. You're all dancing and being silly. It's easy. Everywhere you look there are single guys with corresponding single girls. Dating isn't something you worry about or have to shop for online. It's something you just do. There are the typical heartbreaks that sends a pack of girls into a huddle to cry over. But its normal when you're 25 and single, to date and break up and move on. You are young, and the truth is, you're selfish. You do what you want, when you want, and that selfishness is normal. Expected.

And then one day you wake up Single. But you're staring down 50. And you didn't plan for this. You planned to grow old with someone that loved and respected you. Or you didn't plan at all and woke up Single and thought.... what the heck happened while I was in the coma, I called Marriage?

No one ends up Single because they were seeking Single, Again. They end up Single because they needed to leave a life that was no longer livable. It's the craziest thing when life spins you around and the wheel lands on....

Tinder.

And you ask...what the h@#k is Tinder?

Single, Again
March 25

The beautifully choreographed dance continued as women floated into Single, girl's life. Immediately she knew that the pain she felt would have a purpose. She understood the glazed look of eyes that can never meet another's. Windows to a soul that's been boarded up and nailed shut. A shaking hand that picks up a bottle, lifts it to her nose, as she says, "I don't know what to buy him. He's cheating on me." Behind those eyes lies a photograph of a family with shattered glass.

In front of those eyes would be a woman with compassion, who understands the fear and rejection and confusion.

Feel my love and know...you're never alone.

Single, Again
March 27

The skinny blonde had gone missing. Summer came, and the beach called her name. We kept in touch by text and the occasional coffee with selfies and compliments. We would pretend she still worked there and post pictures on Facebook. The truth she was really there because we had to talk about Romance.

It's funny, you learn a lot about your relationships when you're talking to a friend. It's like opening a closet and taking out the items you've seen a million times but seeing them for the first time. For as much as my BFF had rescued me from my marriage, his own scars were deep. Dating at 50 meant dating after battle, dating with armor on. It was being afraid to give in because you have already sacrificed so much of yourself.

As much as I thought I could pick up and move on after I left my marriage, I would need time to heal. I would make impulsive mistakes and I would be hurtful. My BFF was part of my separation, he was affected by my choices, and by the summers end, he no longer trusted me. At the end of August, we would break up for the last time.

Three weeks later I turned the corner and there she was. My skinny blonde was back on the pay roll.

Single, Again
March 28

It was never a case that married girl was "so strong." She just didn't live with the expectation that her marriage, or the world, was responsible for her happiness. From the depth of her soul, she believed it was her life mission to bring the happiness from her heart into the world.

My candle.
My flame.
My light.

When you can't find the sunshine,
Be the sunshine.

Single, Again
March 28

EVERYTHING
IS GOING
TO BE OK
IN THE END.
IF IT'S NOT
OK, IT'S
NOT THE END.

Single, Again
March 29

The door slides open and she enters the room. The walls and ceiling are white and the floor bare. As she walks into the center of the room, butterflies dance in her stomach. Her eyes follow the length of the walls, and she spins on her heels taking in the entire room in one breath. There are windows on all four walls, without dressing. The sunlight is bursting through on one wall and the dark night on the next. The sky sparkles with diamond stars, endless bursts of hope and energy.

She leaves the window and sits cross-legged on the floor. She imagines the walls pink and then yellow, then blue...shades of the ocean, tones of the beach. She imagines a sofa, two chairs, a big table with seats for everyone she loves. Fabrics in vibrant colors outlining the windows to the world. She giggles.

These are her walls...this is her floor...this is her room. This is her life. She gets to choose.

The possibilities are endless.

Freedom

Single, Again
April 1

The arrival of the skinny blonde back on the scene was mind blowing. Think about it. She had been fired for abandoning her job for a tan and now they were begging her to come back? Just as I became single, again...for the second time.

It took six months of convincing before she agreed to return, and I didn't even know they were asking. When I first saw her in the store, I assumed she was shopping, but when she turned around, she was selling. Was my life scripted?

To truly understand the importance of the skinny blonde you would have to know her and appreciate me. What's more is the irony of Us. Four years before when I was "happily" married, and she became single, I was her pilot on the sanity plane. That was one difficult plane to fly, let me tell ya. Now I was standing in front of her, the teacher. My jaw dropped because she was teaching me survival tips and finishing her sentence with, "I learned that from you, silly!!" She did????

At that point in my life, I completely and totally get how people decide to never date again. It's terrifying. I wasn't using apps for anything, never mind finding a decent man. I didn't order clothing online, or do Peapod, or surf the internet. I did laundry, made peanut butter and jelly, and carpooled. This whole world was going on around me and I had no idea it existed. Bumble? Isn't that a tuna? For all the times I heard commercials for Match and e-harmony, I never once listened. I didn't know they were Real.

My life felt like that nightmare when you show up somewhere important and you're totally naked. I was 100% exposed and 100% vulnerable. Being a woman is never more different than being a man than when you start dating. Women are expected to have babies, work full time, and never age or gain weight. Panic sets in when you realize that you are human, and Mr. Wonderful is going to find your flaws. Mr. Wonderful with the dad bod he's grown to love.

You look in the mirror for the first time in 20 years. Not only have you aged, but hair now grows where you don't want it and falls out where you do. Victoria's Secret...was a secret. I didn't have the secret handshake to go in, and things needed to be pushed up, separated, and have lace. I needed to look brand new, in a way that looked like I Have Always Been Like This.

The truth is, every penny I have made up to this point has gone to care for the three sets of brown eyes that are watching my every move.

I handed over the keys to the insanity plane, and the skinny blonde took the wheel.

Single, Again
April 2

Stephen was a regular at Saks. He was not a shopper, but a guy with a bad attitude who delivered pizza from the food court in the mall. He would pass by a few times a week which allowed us to get used to his snarky nature, until his vision started to deteriorate. There was nothing the doctors could do, and all attempts to save his sight were eventually lost. One day he came in after a trip to the Shaw's across the street. His sight was nearly gone. I asked why he didn't get a nurse to bring him out to run his errands? How could he manage to pay? How was this safe? He leaned in and asked if I was really his friend? "I'm homeless. I live in the bus station down the street." It was absolutely impossible for me to imagine a homeless blind man walking the streets of Boston alone. I thought and thought and thought…and within seconds had a plan.

I reached out to a friend who will forever have a place in my heart. You knew when you met him that he was Someone. He was a tall, thin Irishman with a big family, a thick Boston accent, a strong handshake ….and an even stronger hug. I knew he would help me. He had been a State Senator and had earned the respect of the community.

I spent a lot of time on Stephen, walking him to the train, meeting with agencies, seeking the right home for him. Sometimes I would be walking back from the train station and I would be struck by the irony of my seeking a home for a blind man. Was he very different from me?

Eventually I would find him a home, a place of safety, an escape. And he would turn it down. He would be forced out of the bus station onto the street instead. When the door opens, when there is a hand reaching out for you, when you have a chance, when there is hope, take it. How many of us stay when the obvious choice is to run?

Last year, the front page of the Boston Globe showed a picture of my dear friend, the Senator, who lost his battle with cancer. How many times did I think to call but didn't? I replayed the voice messages over and over on my phone to hear his voice. I imagined his face, felt his hugs. I had not spoken to him in three months, he was one of the prices I paid to change jobs and grow.

I once asked him, "Why do you like me so much?" He wanted me to believe in love, great loves. I hope he's watching me now....

Single, Again
April 3

I am racing through Grand Central Station to catch the train back to Boston when something so familiar catches my eye, and I cannot believe what I am seeing. I don't know what to do, I honestly do not know what to do. I look again and then I keep going, but I know that the image will haunt me for a long time. This will be the first time I walk away from him.

Stephen. My blind, homeless friend. No matter how badly I wanted a better life for him, he had to want it for himself.

The Anatomy of Change.

Single, Again
April 4

I am surrounded in darkness and all I can hear is the tap tap tapping of the long stick that is in my right hand helping me feel my way. With my left hand I reach out, seeking something that will give me a clue…where am I? How did I get here? I call out…hello? …and the echo of my voice flows across the path in front of me. Silence answers, letting me know I am alone. My feet continue down the path, the tap tap tap comforting me in a strange and methodical way. I am not afraid of the darkness or the solitude. I'm just curious. I take a deep breath and send a whisper out to the universe….

"How long have I been blind?"

Single, Again
April 5

Run faster. Run faster. Run faster. Her heart is pounding and hands shaking as she races to the door she cannot wait to open. She is holding a large silver ring filled with keys of all different sizes, shapes, and metals. The faster she runs the more the keys sing. Sing more. Sing more.

The keys fumble in her hands as she tries to find the right key to fit the lock. The journey back to move forward is in her hands. This has to be the one, she feels it in her heart and soul, as it slides completely in and turns. She pushes the door open, the weight of the heavy wood nothing against her desire. Run faster. Run faster.

Down the hall she races to the next door, the keys singing at her hip. This one is gray, the wood chipping off as if it's as ready to be gone as she is. She finds the key, it is long and ornate and rusted. Fragile. She is eager but wise, and carefully slides the key into the lock. A drop of sweat slides down her neck, as the key turns and she realizes that she is no longer alone. Waiting by the door is a woman with dark hair and beautiful smile. She feels the unconditional love and warmth of her dearest friend, her earth angel. They weave their hands together and run to the next door. The woman takes the ring of keys from her and chooses the most beautiful key she has ever seen. For a moment she stares at it, admiring the hearts that are linked one into another, before easily opening the door. The glow of the woman melts into her heart and Together they continue to run down the path.

Waiting outside the next door is a man with soft blue eyes and beard. He is patiently sitting beside the door, reading a comic book and eating a cookie. He smiles at her and she races to his arms. He tells her not to worry, he's got this key, and we are almost there. She feels his peaceful energy drift into her as she races through the door and continues to run.

The path is growing darker, and with each door she finds someone waiting. Someone who made the door capable of being opened. Someone who is now part of her. This is part of healing, meeting people whose love helps you to open the doors to your heart, so you can love again. These walls no longer serve you, you want to feel love and give love. And trust. And be trusted. She throws her arms out and looks up at the sky above her and thanks the universe for the life she has.

And she runs, in complete faith that the last door is within reach...through the darkness until she is standing right in front of its massiveness. On the other side she can hear the methodical sound of the tap tap tapping of a cane. Behind her all of the doors and the path disappear and she is standing in the sunlight of the most beautiful garden she has ever seen. She places both hands flatly on the door and a wave of energy flows through her. All of the love and compassion and gratitude she has collected along the path turn the door into a fine mist. On the other side, the woman with the stick looks up in amazement. 25-year-old me.... you found me.

Single, Again
April 7

25-year-old me took the cane from my hand and whipped it into the forest it came from. She hooked her arm in mine and gently explained, "You were never blind, you were just looking at yourself through the wrong eyes. You couldn't see all that you are because you were feeling all that you thought you were not. Even when you didn't think you were listening to him the words found their way to your eyes." She bent over and filled her hands with water from the stream. "Look", she said, "and when you see your reflection, think Love".

We walked back the way she came, arm in arm, visiting all of the wonderful people who had danced into my life at the exact moment I needed them. Love heals, gratitude heals. She filled her mind with all of the thoughts that make the body flourish, despite what is going on in the world. The eyes are simply the windows, it is your mind that decides what the image means.

25-year-old me took me in her arms and whispered in my ear, "We learned everything we need to know. Our vision is perfect."

It was now time to fall in love.

Single, Again
April 8

My 50th birthday…my entire family celebrating in my paradise…Maine. My sister hands me a card with a life changing gift….

We bought you an angel reading….

Single, Again
April 9

My angel reading was scheduled for March 2017…nine months after my birthday!!! She is that good and that busy. I am flat out a 100% believer in all things Angels. I've read countless books on near-death experiences and I truly believe there is more to life than what we see before us. I was so incredibly excited!! I couldn't imagine waiting all that time and as fate would have it, I was going to get a preview. The angel reader invited my sister to a group reading in November at a golf club near her house. We decided it would be a blast to go with her daughters, and I am sure not one person at the event walked in more fired up than me.

There were chairs set up in rows with an aisle up the center. Because we mingled too long over the buffet, the 5 of us were separated. I insisted that my sister and I sat together. My two nieces found seats directly behind us, and one niece sat alone on the other side of the room. At the start of the event the reader said, "Not everyone is going to get a reading. Please listen to what I say to others because there could be a message in there for you." I grasped my hands together and thought "Pick me!"

She started doing readings on the other side and I kept encouraging myself to be happy for the other people. Listen. And I truly was. There was a woman who lost her husband, he had been young and the death sudden. The reader brought her peace. Then she asked to the person in the back of the room if she had more time? They said yes, a few more minutes. She closed her eyes and bowed her head. Then she looked at me and said, "The blonde woman in the white shirt, what is your name?" The sound of my voice coming from my throat sounded foreign. "There is a man behind you. He is connected to you through your father. He is all dressed up, and he doesn't usually dress like this, but he was so excited to be here. He shined his shoes and everything. He wants you to know there is a man in your life and he was made for you". My heart was racing. The skinny blonde had introduced me to her friend, the train guy, and I couldn't imagine he was made for me? She continued, despite my confusion. "He loves watching you together. He even reminds him of himself. And he loves your children. There are so many exciting things that are going to happen. He goes like this." She leans back like she's taking off on a rollercoaster. Then she closes her eyes again, to listen, and when she opens her eyes, she shakes her head and says, "Yes, he says it's your husband. He wants you to know he was made for you." The whole room says "Awwww".

Except me.

I turned to my sister in shock, wondering how could it be that I came for clarity but what I heard was a riddle? "What does that mean?" The size of her eyes said she had no idea. I turned around to my nieces whose shoulders lifted in unison, their palms to the sky. The couple sitting to the right of me were staring at the woman with the beautiful reading who was clearly freaking out. Imagine a man being made for me? My husband? I explained, "There is no husband. Well, there was one. Oh my god, was he made for me?"

I can just picture my uncle behind me, completely freaking out over my translation to his words. "No, no, no…do not move on to another reading!!! Oh my God! Come back to her!!!" He stood there and watched me get up, probably pushed me out of the chair, and walk up to the Angel Reader. I couldn't stop myself.

"I don't understand. There is no husband." I knew what I was doing wasn't fair to her or the others in the room. Her response was kind, but short. "Think of all of the men in your life. You just really need to think." And then she was gone.

I decided she was talking about my youngest son. How else would I be able to sleep?

Single, Again
April 10

The skinny blonde showed up on the scene with a little black book and a sly smile. She had a friend, would love to set me up, what did I want from a man? That's a loaded question. All I could say was I just wanted a man who had already done all the work on himself. Tall, short, rich, poor, I really did not care. I just wanted to start with something simple: peace.

She gave him my number and he sent a few texts. In full disclosure, I was unprepared in every way. I realized this in the exact second my phone was ringing, and I knew I had to speak. To a stranger. "Sooooooo the skinny blonde...." he said. Every pore on my body opened and within seconds I was dehydrated. He was nice. We made a date. I blew him off. I felt bad, petrified, unsure. I sent a text. He pretended to not know it was me. I bought his joke. He said, "I am having dinner tonight at Bella's if you want to come." I tossed my phone on the seat of my car. Now what have I done? I had to go. Are you kidding me?

The drive to meet a stranger feels transatlantic. There is no GPS from the car to the date. You literally go into autopilot and pray for your survival. "What's the big deal?" The skinny blonde says. "It's just dinner." I knew he was out there. I just had to find the courage to find him.

Single, Again
April 11

What I love about my life is that I can start a sentence by saying, "What I love about women is…" I meet women every day who impress upon my mind and my heart the need for our bond. The absolute necessity that we support each other on our journeys, that we have compassion for what it means to be a mother, a home maker, and a full-time employee. It's a lot. And we do it.

What I love about women is that connection that comes from raw communication, vulnerable, 'I get you' honesty. I love when I haven't heard from you in a while and you say, "I miss you more than you know." We pick up where we left off, because we simply paused. And in that pause, I still felt you.

I love women for their woven vulnerability and strength, the depths of our thoughts, our courage in feeling more than is comfortable. And what I love about women is that we aspire to be more than we are because of our mothers, and grandmothers, and great-great grandmothers…we are the ever-evolving gender.

If you're reading this…and you get me…know that what I love about women is that it can be more than enough just knowing you're there…and I'm here.

Single, Again
April 12

In the beginning I couldn't get out of my own way. The skinny blonde insisted that being single was easy and fun but internally, I was a train wreck. We made a date to go out to dinner after work one night, just the two of us, for an icebreaker. Full disclosure: I felt guilty not going home to my kids. I felt self-conscious about every part of my being…. that feeling you get when you are walking away, and you know someone is staring at you. I had no idea how to walk into a crowded bar and pretend like I belong there. I was a socially awkward 50-year-old.

The skinny blonde ran the city like a pro. She ordered cosmos shaken violently and I thought …just hand the glass to me… (shaking violently). We ended up with two seats at Joe's for dinner. Apparently, people eat at the bar? The bartender knew her, placed her regular order for us to split, and I ordered a Corona Light with lime. The entire night I never took my eyes off her, never acknowledged the room full of strangers, never let the ice break.

She had been pushing Tinder for 2 years now. "Don't be silly, just sign-up. Everyone is on it, it's attached to Facebook. C'mon it's fun!" Hmmm. She was the expert and she said it would be Fun? Fine. Fine? I guess it's fine. How bad can it be?

When I got home, I grabbed my iPad, took a gigantic breath, and signed up. Tinder pulled all of my information from Facebook, which in the moment was kind of comforting. Until I woke up at 2am in a full body sweat because I just posted everything about me to a world of strangers.

I deleted the account.

Single, Again
April 13

She hovered at the edge of the cloud, looking down at the vast world beneath her. Everywhere her eyes went there was motion. A butterfly, a car, a bike, two people side by each in a boat, hugging. Where would she land? How would it feel, finally, to have dewy grass hide between her toes? She pulled back for a moment and turned her attention to her master far above her, yet right by her side. There was a purpose to her journey...a calling from above to leave her mark on what was below. She would grow there...not always easily. Some of her growth would come at a cost, a temporary ache at times and at others a call of courage to forge forward. From above came a light, a multi-colored beam of warmth, shining down on her and letting her know that everything would be alright. It was what was meant to be.

She took one more glimpse at the flickering of lights from the world below. The mist of the cloud engulfed her as she slipped from its comfort, the beam of multi-colored light wrapping itself around her and carrying her safely to the place where she would rest...her mother's arms.

Life

Single, Again
April 15

She arrived in her mother's arms, a single soul, with a single journey of infinite possibilities. Single is how we arrive, and Single is how we depart. Single means complete ownership of choices and decisions, successes and failures. Single means owning her story, recognizing that her choices impact others, but her obligation is to her soul.

She arrived single, and then one day, married. Marriage was a contract...an agreement to behave in a certain way over time. Two people, living side by side, as individuals, held together by a document. An obligation.

She arrived in her mother's arms with a story to write. Of infinite possibilities. She looked back up at the sky, through the clouds, to where her master watched from above. She came here to love...a single candle.

And she would glow.

Single, Again
April 16

I told the skinny blonde I would bring my iPad to work so she could teach me how to use Tinder. She told me to go on Pinterest and watch the tutorial. I didn't know how to tell her I didn't have Pinterest, so I tossed the iPad on the pillow beside me and fell asleep. Until the panic attack at 2:30am when I deleted my account. I was totally sure that when I got to work, my coworkers would tell me to keep it off.

It turns out that all day long my coworkers were working Tinder. The guys loved it!!! It was just one of many apps they used to meet each other. And it was NORMAL to them. "Oh, all you do is look at the picture and then swipe right if you like them and left if you don't." Are you kidding me? "If you swipe up there are more pictures and some people write things." I used to hear these small moans from across the room that sounded like "ughhhh". It turns out that it meant someone swiped left instead of right and the love of their life was gone. Just like that.

I'll admit that my biggest problems were that I believed that if love was meant to come my way, it would. I was afraid of looking eager and desperate like I was selling myself on an online tag sale. And worst of all, I didn't know how to make myself take it lightly. How could I shake up my guarded self and lower my walls long enough to appear flippant and carefree? Would I ever be able to swipe right, swipe left while waiting in line at Dunkin?

I went home that night and decided I would try one more time. It was almost the new year and my resolution was to fit into my new life. I climbed in my bed and positioned my iPad carefully so there would be no swiping accidents. One by one faces appeared on my screen until I saw this Robbie Benson look-alike staring back at me and I froze. My god, he's so cute. I read his profile…fireman, non-smokers only…a few other facts. I was intrigued. I viewed his other pictures. Why was he single? How bad could a man be who climbs trees to rescue cats and carries people from burning buildings? I swiped right and turned my iPad off.

In the morning I woke up to a message. "I would love to meet you."

He would love to meet me?

Single, Again
April 17

Finding myself single at 50 was never going to feel like it did at 25. Life changed me. And the people I would meet had been journeying for quite some time before bumping into me. We all have scars from living. I remember my dad used to get in the car and drive to work, work all day, call my mom from the office, and then drive home. Normal was coming home and sitting on the couch and talking about their day. I can't imagine my dad tweeting or my mom getting upset because of a picture she saw on my dad's Facebook. Private Relationships have become very Public. And I think it's hard on us. Texting has made it easy to say things impulsively and read them in the tone of our choice. My parents never had to Block anyone...or unfriend them...the concept would have been ridiculous.

I began dating, thinking I would figure it out with time. I wanted to be happy, I wanted to find my laugh. Dating is teaching me how important communication is to me...and I am finding my happy place...but I had it backwards.

You don't find yourself by dating. You find your-self, and then date.

Single, Again
April 18

I walked in a daze back to my chair and plopped down next to my sister. "She couldn't tell me anything. I don't get it." I could see in her eyes what she couldn't say. She wanted this night to help me. I had been through so much and this was MY everything. I wanted answers. I wanted to understand, to make sense of what happened before and what would happen next. I decided to shake it off, and really enjoy the next speaker.

The next speaker was my angel readers mentor and drove in from a town on the South Shore of MA. She told her story, of losing her sister, and how her death led her to angel reading. Then she said, "Jennifer showed you how she can bring the spirits to you and now I am going to show you how to do that for yourself."

We were sitting on hard, metal fold out chairs, and I had my small plate of food and glass of water at my feet. She had us close our eyes and began what would be my first meditation. "The room is filled with only kind spirits, so close your eyes and invite them to come to you." Instantly I felt tears start to fall from my eyes, and I thought, "Oh my god, does anyone know I am crying?" I followed her voice and did what she said. Invite them to come to you and try to see them. I felt a rush of the most incredible outpouring of love and compassion flood the center of my body. I felt as if I was being hit by a wave. I couldn't stop it from happening, and I didn't want it to. Even though I was elbow-to-elbow in a strange room, I was experiencing the most intimate moment of my life. I searched for the faces of my angels, but only saw darkness. Everything came to me in words.

"You are so loved" was their message. They, who knew everything. They, who I could not hide from. They, who saw straight through me and filled the enormous empty part of my soul with their light. I could not believe this was happening. The love they sent was so intense that I ached. She brought us out of the meditation.

I needed to leave. We found our way out of the country club and to my sister's car. I cried so passionately hard, that I couldn't speak. I felt as if I had emptied all of the pain of my marriage from my soul. There love opened me, and in the pain, it healed me. And my greater truth is that for the first time, I could not deny a thing.

I walked into my sister's house looking like a drowned rat. My son looked at me and asked, "How was it?"

I would begin regular meditations the next day.

Single, Again
April 19

Vulnerability

"Be careful", she said. "He might hurt you."

"Oh mom, there is always the chance that tomorrow he might hurt me. But today, he's making me happy. I can't reserve my happiness for another day when I have the chance today."

Single, Again
April 20

Safety

My earliest memory is of waking up in my crib. The room was dark, and it was quiet. I sat up in my bed and waited, hoping someone would come and scoop me up into their arms. I remember seeing the light along the door frame, the door slowly opening. He whispers to me, the gentle talk of a parent to a waking child. He reaches in, lifts me to his face, and I rest my head on his shoulder.

My father.

Single, Again
April 21

Trust was never going to come easily for me, and I honestly didn't even know who I was. I had become this oversized chocolate Easter bunny, a hollow one, with a molded grin and sugar glazed eyes. I took the chocolate bunny on dates, let him meet the outside. I listened politely to the train guy talk about his broken family, and then the fireman. The Tinder fireman with the tragic childhood he would never really be able to recover from and have a normal relationship. I recognized with the fireman a familiarity that I could not live with but was drawn to. He couldn't love, and I was used to that. He talked, and I listened, and I don't think he ever thought to himself, "I know nothing about her."

I'm not sure at the time I really knew what I could ask for from a man. What did I want? I wanted to be able to be myself, the real me, without hesitation or fear. I wanted…ughhh…I wanted fun and happiness and I wanted a friendship caught on fire. I wanted a man to really love me when I wasn't pretending to be exactly what he wanted. I wanted to be the solid Easter bunny.

I went to bed and cut all kinds of deals with my angels.

Single, Again
April 22

Delicate is the heart that understands,
She seeks not what she can find under the stars,
But within her soul....
A treasure to be given
Love

Single, Again
April 23

2017

The one who felt like Meryl Streep at the Emmys yelled across the aisle, "Hey, single girl.... I have a date tonight!" Meryl had recently lost some weight, won a few sales awards, and was feeling good about herself. I told her not to forget to behave and she said that if everything went well, she was planning to book a few hours at the American Hair Removal Institute of Mass. the next day. "It's an all-day appointment." I adore Meryl...she's beautiful, smart, and funny. The fact that she is alone means she is robbing someone of the pleasure of her company. I was (maybe) a bit more excited than her.

The next day I came to work and raced to hear...

"Well, we met at the bar of this amazing Italian restaurant. He was very handsome, and the conversation was great. He asked if I wanted to get a table and eat. I thought...I'm starving...but I said, 'I guess, if you want to.' So, we got a table. I ordered the Risotto with shrimp. It was a special. As the food arrived, he asked if I had read his profile? I said I had, of course. You're divorced. Then he said, "Well...."

You can see where this is going?

"Well, I'm not exactly divorced. We just separated two weeks ago. We are testing separation." Meryl mentally cancelled Hair Removal. "What are you doing with me then? I am not your test market. Did you read MY profile?"

Meryl looked at her delicious dinner and then at the man who had lured her here because he likes women and wants to have some fun. She stood up, put on her coat, and picked up the shrimp risotto.

"You'll have to explain to the waitress about the bowl." And walked out.

Single, Again
April 24

When we last left off about my angel reader, there was a man standing behind me who came to me through my father. He was uncomfortably dressed, in a suit and shined shoes, eager and so excited to be there. This man is my uncle. I knew it instantly. He was 16 years old the day he became my God Father. He was a dude, wore his curly hair long, and listened to the Beatles on 8-track tapes in his car. I remember the day he passed. It was Thanksgiving and I had run the Manchester Road Race and loved it. Some runs make me feel like I am flying, free as a bird, and this run was like that. I learned that he lost his battle to lung cancer when I got home. He was only 42 years old. The fact that he was eager to talk to me about a man, let me know that all of my angels were listening to me cut deals at night. He said, "I want you to know there is a man in your life and he was made for you." Twice she said, with emphasis, Made for You!

I'm sitting on my bed with my iPad on my lap, a full year and a half later, and I am still in disbelief....

Someone was made? For me???

Single, Again
April 25

What if?

What if you met someone who wanted to hear all of your thoughts and dreams? And share his with you?

What if there was someone who wasn't afraid to share you with the world? Trusted you to drift out and come back? Encouraged friendships...watered the seed that is you?

What if you met a man who couldn't imagine not walking you to the car? Smiled as you drove away? Called to make sure you were safe?

What if...you didn't settle. Didn't make excuses. Didn't justify. Didn't think this is all that there is?

What if...you allowed yourself to be the princess that you are? Let yourself be loved, adored, cherished, trusted.

Oh my God, what if?

Single, Again
April 27

Dear Self,

What if it were okay to make a mistake? What if forgiving yourself set you free? What would happen if you realized you have no one to answer to but you? Would you dance in your kitchen? Would you paint each of your nails a different color? Wear your favorite dress to the market?

What if there were no rules to this game of life? Would you worry less and sing more? There's going to come a day, that has already come, when you can be who you are without regret. What if knowing that made you giggle?

What if...life was meant to be an unscripted, unedited, unrehearsed, untitled story....and the pen could have any color ink you choose? Would you fill your pages with pink ink? Would you smile as you turned the pages of your story?

I look in the mirror, and there she is. Self....would it be okay...if I hug you?

XO,

Me

Single, Again
April 28

2014
Discipline

When I first discovered the affair, I was a horrible cocktail of shock and denial. It's the things that we never see coming that knock us down the hardest. We lose our sense that "what we see is what is." It's like being blindsided at an intersection, and then you start to drive like everyone might hit you. I sought things that gave me a sense of control. If I could not stop what was happening, maybe I could at least slow it down. Just enough so that I could catch up with it.

Life doesn't stop just because you have been devastated by a broken heart, a traumatized life, a shattered home. There is no set cure for a woman who wakes up and looks at the pillow beside her and wonders how he can possibly be gone? A shattered life is in the hands of the shattered. Initially I became a Stepford Wife, methodically providing immaculate service to a man...who was just a man.

As I processed what was going on, my mind would spin, and I couldn't believe he had stolen my life. My twenties, my thirties, my forties...this was time I would never get back. I would be making beds thinking, "He stole my youth. He haphazardly and without a care in the world, redefined every memory I have." I had to forcefully shake myself. I had to create the vision of a dark forest and keep my mind from going there. I came to realize the discipline of getting out of bed every morning. The affair was a bump in the road, it wasn't the road. And it wasn't my bump.

I would come to understand that every single thing we do requires Discipline.

Single, Again
April 29

I walked into the Angel Readers office and she said, "Have I ever done a reading for you before?" I explained about the event in November, when we met my uncle. Let's be honest, waiting 6 months to get an explanation about this man that was made for me was a true act of patience! I would now have a full hour alone with my reader and my angels. For everything I ever wanted this hour to be, I could never have been prepared. "I was hoping you could explain that to me?", I said in a voice I barely recognized. She nodded and asked if I brought my phone?

"You'll want to tape this."

The secret to life is knowing that there is a secret to life.

Single, Again
May 1

I returned with my phone, set it to record our conversation and forgot it was there. She asked me to place my hands-on top of hers and she began with a prayer inviting my angels into the room. During the darkest days of my married life, I felt the presence of someone helping me and I would close my eyes and say, "Please show me who you are. I just want to thank you." I would close my eyes, expecting to see my grandmother. Or her sister. I would learn on this day that my angel reading was a conversation with my guardian angels and that they had revealed themselves to me one night in a dream. They were the colored lights streaming down from my ceiling…. the archangels were the colors with my guardian angel in the center. "That was not a dream," my angel reader said, "that's how they come to you. And they know you are grateful."

The reading began as if she had been hiding behind me my entire married life. She knew everything, right down to the timing. As I listen to the tapes play back to me, I can hear myself crying. Another person would think it was pain from my past. But it wasn't.

I could feel their love and compassion so deeply in my heart that I overflowed. There was no hiding from my Angels.

And no desire to hide.

Single, Again
May 2

"It was a lesson for him and it was a lesson for you," she said. The truth is, I already knew that. That was behind me. Now I wanted to know that I was going to be ok. I wanted to hear that I was lovable, that my future would be this explosive firework of laughter and joy. I wanted to believe that I was going to walk out of the ambers into the arms of someone who wanted to spin me around on the dance floor, run with me on the beach, whisper in my ear. I wanted what I never had.

And then she said, "There is a gentleman coming into your life…"

And I wanted to faint. Except I couldn't because then I would miss what she said next.

Single, Again
May 4

Five days earlier....

11:34 pm
I get a text from the skinny blonde....
Her: "What's going on with your love life?"
Me: "Same as before."
Her: "There's a great guy who just became single. He's fresh on the market, just I like I like 'em.... fresh like lobstah."
Me: "What's his name?"
Her: She tells me and then, "Send him a friend request."
Me: "Absolutely not."
Her: "Fine, do it tomorrow."
Me: "He just sent me a request."
Her: laughing
Me: smiling

Single, Again
May 5

"This gentleman that is going to come into your life, I want you to know that it was divinely inspired a long time ago. All I need you to do in order to meet him is to be very open and deserving and know that you deserve to have pleasure in all that you do. I want you to know he is a true gentleman. And I want you to know that at first it will be very hard for you to trust someone.....I just want you to know that when this person comes into your life, it's ok for you to take it slow....I want you to know he is very strong and confident and he has learned a lot from his past....he's a good man."

She gave me a time frame for when he would come into my life. She challenged me to raise my vibrations. "Tell your angels that you are ready. Thank them for putting him into your life even before he gets there. You are deserving and full of love. Tell them, "I can shower someone with my love and they will appreciate me."

She said, "Imagine what it will feel like to wake up to an amazing gentleman, who can't wait to share his life and feelings and ideas with you. Imagine being part of something where he wants you to be involved in his life." Seriously? He is going to come home from work and want to share his day with me? His children with me? I am going to be more than a fixture? And then she said... "You're going to be like...my god, this is so weird. Is this real? Will it last?"

And I burst out laughing.

Single, Again
May 6

I drove home with the Angel readers voice blasting through my car speakers. She said so many things that intrigued and baffled and awed and inspired me. Most of all, she brought me peace. "You need to forgive yourself from that time and for how long it took. They understand, you were protecting, and you were scared." And then she said this...and when I heard it play back to me, I was shocked. "Even the Blessed Mother says, 'you have to tell her that she has to allow herself to forgive herself." Wait a minute, are you serious??? The Blessed Mother knows me?!?!?! At first, I couldn't believe that with all of the people in the world, the Blessed Mother could see me. When I listen back today, I am able to feel her love and to know that I deserve her love.

I am also a Blessed Mother. I am blessed with three incredible young men, who's love carried me along a difficult journey to where I am today. Love was the how and the why. Love is the purpose. Love is the reward.

I believe the Blessed Mother sees every single one of us. She's a Mother...and that's what Mothers do.

Single, Again
May 6

Step 1:
Believe: Thank you for bringing
an amazing man into my life.

May 7

Dear Self,
What do you want from a man?
Love,
Me

Dear Me,
Seriously? I get to ask for stuff?
Love,
Self

PS This is pretty exciting.
Dear Self,
Silly girl…figure out what really makes you happy and then imagine that he's real.
Love,
Me

Manifestation

Single, Again
May 8

I made a comment on one of his pictures and he sent me a private message. He wants to go for a walk on the beach near his house. I message back that I've never met a beach I didn't like. He writes back, I write back, I scan a few of his pictures and read some of his posts.

I send his name to my sister in Connecticut. What do you think of this guy? She is my touch stone, and she's been with me every step of the way. I guess we will talk more about it when I go to my angel reading next week. Something about him catches her eye and she does some research. She watches some YouTube videos and listens to his life story. By the time I get to her house, she's a fan.

She asks me if I have watched the videos? Seriously? "There are videos?"

After the Angel Reading, I drop myself in one of her chairs and log onto YouTube.

Single, Again
May 9

Him: "Hey, I feel like a couple of teenagers texting all the time. Would it be ok if I called you?"

Me: "I don't think so."

I listened to everything my reading told me over and over again. It was that moment in my life when I had to see exactly what I wanted and truly believe I was worthy of it. He had mentioned that he was spending time with happy women with good attitudes, walking on the beach. I didn't want to be one of many, even though I understood where he was at in his life.

Him: "Why?"

Me: "Because I am looking for a car and you are offering a bike. I think you're worth waiting for, so I will wait for the car."

Another month passed, and he asked, "When can I meet you?"

"When you ask."

Tomorrow it will be one year since he decided to offer the car.

Single, Again
May 14

The plan for the date is to begin with Hot Yoga, followed by kayaking to an island with a picnic lunch, a long walk on the beach, and a $10 tour of his town.

We wake up to a Nor'easter.

The biggest problem with the Nor'easter isn't the kayaks, it's my hair. The minute my hair knows it's going to rain, I become Diana Ross. And if I try to tame it by putting it in a ponytail, suddenly I'm going to gym class. And the whole make-up thing became confusing...do I wear makeup to hot yoga or show up looking like I have the flu? Mascara has this way of sliding from my eyelashes to my chin and to be honest...I need lipstick. I blow-dry my hair, dress for yoga, and put on enough make up to look alive.

When I arrive, 30 minutes late because GPS took me on a scenic route, we have now missed hot yoga. He lives in a condo along a marina that faces Boston in the distance. Even in the midst of a storm, it's relaxing. As I parked my car, I stopped worrying about my hair and my make-up and my yoga pants.

Today was about my heart.

Single, Again
May 14

I walk into his condo and all I can smell is coconut and vanilla. The view out every window is of the ocean, and I don't really know what to look at first. So, I drift around looking at his books and signs, the softness of the colors, the photos of his family and friends. He asks if I would like a cappuccino? And I say "Sure, that sounds terrific and very Italian". I find my way to his desk. I sit in his chair and look out to the ocean. "You must get a lot of work done here," I joke.

But what I am thinking is, what would it be like to hug a man who was made for me? Divinely decided a long time ago? Will I know it when our hands touch? Will I melt in his arms?

I have waited my entire life. She told me to just be my authentic self, that is what he is going to be drawn to. At the time we laughed because my angels said, "She doesn't even know who she is yet." She wants to know. She wants to let go…and she knows it is up to her to crack the shell and grow.

So, I get up from his desk and walk to the kitchen where he is making coffee. He turns to me, smiles, and says, "What?" And I can't answer with words. I take one more step and wrap my arms around him.

And now I know what it feels like to be in the arms of the man who was made for me.

Single, Again
May 14

The only thing on the date check list that we could do was the $10 tour. We climbed into his made for sunshine car and made our way down the streets of his town. The homes in this old beach town are beautiful, even in the rain, and I was really digging the tour. Suddenly he pulled the car over and thought for just a second. He shook his head and said, "Yes, I have to show you the view from here." We get out of the car and walk toward the ocean, my hair blowing horizontally across my face. The ocean was violently crashing into the coast and it was invigorating!!! What a view!!!

As we turn to leave, I see a staircase heading down to the beach and say, "Hey, let's go put our feet in the water!!" I'm not sure if this is a good idea or a bad idea, but I can't stop myself. At the foot of the stairs, we are standing on a large rock, both of us now barefoot. The ocean is as aggressive as I have ever seen it, but the water isn't making it to my feet. He pulls out his phone and starts to take a Mother's Day Video. All I want is wet feet. Hmmm, how can I do this? I turn my head to the left and see water running down the rock wall. Should I just stick my toes under there? At that exact second, I turn back to the ocean and a wave crashes on a rock, flying up in the air, and smacks me right in the face.

I am now screaming, "Oh my God did you see that!!" to the man with the video camera I don't want to be on. I am laughing so hard I can barely breathe, and my clothes are now stuck to my body and my bangs are pasted to my forehead. The filming ends and I grab him by both his arms and say…. "Look at me!!!!"

We return to his car and I can't believe I am sitting on his leather seats when I am drenched in salt water. He doesn't seem to mind, and I love that. The heat and my moisture level fog the windows, but I am able to see in the rear-view mirror that my mascara is 6 inches below my eye. I try to discreetly wipe my eyes and simultaneously squeeze curls into my hair without him noticing. And then he says….

"Oh my God!!! How lucky are we!!! There's my brother!!! Let's get out and talk to him!!" Are you kidding me????? He lives in Vermont!!!! I slurp from the car like a swamp lizard and pray his brother has no sense of smell and poor eyesight. I wonder who I think I am walking into a beautiful beach home with my webbed feet and seaweed outfit.

The only words I managed to say to his brother are, "I got hit by a wave." He smiles.

Our next stop is a military site that was created a gazillion years ago and is super cool and definitely worthy of the $10 tour. We are standing on a hill overlooking Boston and the wind picks up its pace and severity. I have never felt so free, never felt so alive.

I start to jump up and down because I am so excited, I can't stand still. The only thing I can think to do is hug him and laugh into his neck, "I am soooo happy!"

Best date in the history of the world.

Single, Again
June 1

It would be their third or fourth date when he started calling her "Bella".

The sunrise and the sunset were part of his daily ritual, and his home was positioned perfectly to watch the day end in brilliance. She came from work, dressed in her uniform of all black, topped with an invisible cloak of protection she had self-stitched over the years. They made a date to watch the sunset together from his deck facing Boston. The bay is filled with boats and children are jumping into the water from the pier. She turned the corner and there he was, waiting for her....in his uniform of a rich tan, crisp linen shirt, and smile that went from his heart to his lips.

They climbed the three flights of stairs, chatting the whole way about the silly things that happened during the day. And then he opened the door. The song she had been researching the day before was playing on Alexa, making her head spin...had he really been listening to her? Walking into his home she wanted to cry at the amount of time and energy he had put into making this moment perfect. Did she really mean this much to him? The lights were set to sparkling candlelight, the scent of vanilla and coconuts drawing her in, beautiful flowers set in vases, and then she looked through the glass doors. "There is wine and strawberries with chocolate waiting on the deck", he said, so softly she thought she dreamt it.

Both of her hands instinctively went to her head. "You're going to have to go slowly with me. I don't know how to take all of this in at once."

She would have to learn to believe that what she was seeing was real.

Single, Again
June 2

There is no greater time of vulnerability than when you are falling in love. The truth is that it appears to be easier to manage a relationship that is Average than one that is Everything You've Ever Wanted. Average allows every guard you've ever created to stay intact, and if necessary, grow. Average means that if things are going well, and you're having fun, the relationship appears perfect. Appears perfect. Average is volatile because the second something goes astray, you're done. It's like being at Six Flags screaming on a rollercoaster one second and the next it starts to pour and you're running for your car, wanting your money back. Accepting Less Than, becomes the dance of breaking up and getting back together. It's the dance of making excuses for bad behavior, for telling your friends it's over and then getting back together. It's believing the moments that draw you back in are bigger than the ones that pull you apart. It is a trap that is created by the fear of having Everything You Have Ever Wanted, or not believing that type of love exists.

Bella knew this was what she prayed for when no one was listening but her angels. She prayed for a love and a life she could only imagine. It was a life she would have to build by breaking down who she had become. It wasn't when things were going well that Bella would struggle, it was when the rain started to fall. And she didn't run to the car. And she didn't want her money back. She would give Everything She Ever Wanted... Everything she had.

Single, Again
June 15

She came to dread her birthday, all holidays, in fact, and it never dawned on her how sad this was. It was part of her norm not to have expectations for people, and her birthday was the greatest opportunity for pass/fail. The weeks going into it made her nervous, people bring it up... "Hey, your birthday is coming. What are you going to do?" And then after, "What did he give you?" What did they do? Even the demand...have a Happy Birthday seemed to rock her...so much pressure on everyone. The day after had become her favorite day, when it was over, when she could focus on the birth of her first son.

As a child the parties were enormous, and she would celebrate for a week. Chocolate frosted cupcakes and a little girl with pig tails making the biggest wish possible and blowing with all her might. Her mother would make pizza after pizza, Cheetos and potato chips in bowls on the deck, and they would all sleep over and swim in the pool all night. She would watch the parade from the side of the road and truly believe it was for her. There was the year she got the lime green bean-bag chair, the Loves Baby Soft perfume with the matching T-shirt, a gift set from her sisters. She loved the attention, the laughter, the gifts.... all of it. When did it become such high risk?

They met three weeks before. He talked about her birthday with the excitement he would feel about his own. She tried to temper it, bring him to understand that birthdays weren't for her. She would go to work, have dinner with her boys. And he listened. Not to her, but to himself. He would drive the hour to her job and she would hear his voice ask her coworker, "Isn't she the most beautiful girl in the world?" She would turn, and her heart would drop at the sight of him and he would begin the process of changing how she felt about this day. It didn't matter to him that the past few decades made her dread this day, that was before...before The Stone Story.

In his hand was a gift bag with a box and a poem...

The Stone Story-

"smiles & laughter"

I didn't know there was something missing until I found you.
It was like stumbling upon an unharmed
sand dollar after spending a lifetime
Collecting broken bits of glass.
We are a perfect accident
Brought together by the ebb and flow of
Fate's turquoise tides.

Inside the box she would find a necklace. A perfectly shaped heart of sea glass with a silver sand dollar. He had found it while walking, before they met, and had it made for her.

For her....

Single, Again
June 18

He knew the second she stepped out of the car that something was bothering her. He wrapped both of his arms around her and kissed her gently on the lips. Something was clearly wrong. He took her hand and they started to walk along the bay, the conversation awkward, her body language screaming out, "Make me tell you before I burst!" So, he stops and says, "Bella, I know something is wrong. You gave me that terrible kiss when you got out of the car, and…". She stops him dead in his tracks…did he just say terrible kiss? Seriously? That was all she needed to start to crack, just a little, just enough to get him to see where the kiss came from.

They walked along to the beach, sharing different sides of the same story, working their way to an understanding. He asked her to please take his phone and tape a video for him with the ocean in the background. He wants to know when she is ready, can she really see him and hear him? She gives the thumbs up, she has taped his videos many times before. She presses the red button and he starts to speak with both of his arms out. He is looking right at her through the lens.

"Bella, Bella, Bella…I just want you to know that I love you with all my heart. You are the most loving, kind, sweet, amazing, brilliant woman I have ever met. I love you". She stops the video and looks at this man who now has both of his hands at his heart. She walks to him and kisses him with Everything She's Got. Love, respect, joy, and the hardest of all…. trust.

He sends her the video with a note: If you ever wonder, play this….

May 2017

Bella started to believe in love….

Single, Again
Love Stories

June 19
A Love Story

    I follow my father into the dark room and watch as he lifts me from the crib. My little hands rest on his shoulders and he places his hand on my back, gently rubbing the way a parent does. He will be the first man to love me, to protect me. From my father and my mother, I will learn everything I need to know about love. And then they will set me free.

    I walk over to my father and kiss him on the cheek. He is giggling with her and she is lost in the happiness of his face. He carries me out of the room with the promise that no matter what the future held, he would never put me down.

Single, Again
June 20
A Love Story

It's Sunday night and my son climbs on the bus after an incredible weekend. He looks out the window to see if she is still crying? Goodbye has always been hard on her...and him, too, but in a different way. He settles into his seat and starts to think.

He wants to do something for her. Something so romantic and kind and unexpected that it blows her mind. For the next hour he plays on Google until he has a plan for Monday morning.

He calls the store and explains that his girlfriend lost the pearl earrings her grandmother had given her four years before. She wore them every day. He had them wrapped in the iconic bag every girl adores. "She will be there at 5:30...please enclose a card to read, "Dear Pal, your ears sure did look lonely this weekend." He must have felt all of the explosive joy that true love brings. To her, he sent a text that read "Call me when you leave work."

At 5:00 she stood on the street outside her Manhattan office and called him at his desk in Boston. From google maps to her feet, he directed her to her surprise location. Walk two blocks and take a left...see the Starbucks? Take a right...until finally she arrived at Tiffany's. A gentleman put her in the private elevator and took her to the 6th floor. "This is for you." This little girl in this big city holding this blue bag from this boy who loves her. All of This for her.

I text him…did she cry?
He replies, "Mom, she's still crying!!!"
So was I. My boy….
Love is patient. Love is kind.

Single, Again
June 20

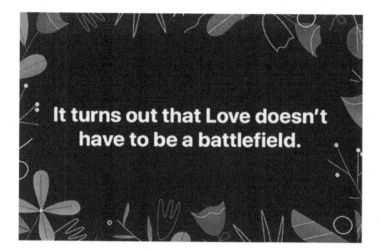

It turns out that Love doesn't have to be a battlefield.

Single, Again
June 21
A Love Story…

She was a freshman cheerleader with an adorable smile and a huge crush. As she climbed the bus for the away game, the senior hockey players would tease her and chant her name. There was one special boy, a naughty, tough goalie with a tremendous spirit. He was the one.

He graduated and went on his crooked path through college, while she continued her years of high school. She was popular and pretty and just the right amount of shy. Life was good for each of them.

One fate blessed night…

They hadn't seen much of each other over the years…separate colleges, same hometown. She is out with her friends, laughing and looking…when suddenly…there he is. His friends will tell the story that he would never stay in one place too long, but on this night, he would not leave. He found Her…She was the one.

They would marry and climb the mountains of life. Children would come, beautiful children with big hearts and contagious smiles. He would only ever have eyes for her and to his friends he would say "Isn't my love the most beautiful girl here?" And she would wake up and say, "I can't believe I married the boy of my dreams."

He was the guy who would hop in the car and take the boys to the Super Bowl…without tickets and get them there. He's the guy jumping out of airplanes, buying race cars. They would go on cruises and to their kids sporting events, start companies and buy real estate. Fearless and full of life.

She would create the warmest most loving home imaginable. A place where everyone would gather, a center for their universe. Here they would live and love and grow and face the ups and the downs.

Life doesn't always make sense. His diagnosis never felt possible. Their journey together was preciously woven, and in this life, she may never understand why his ended first. He is part of every single thing she is, every single thing she loves.

He would change form...we are not our mind, we are not our body...we are Our Spirit. Our spirit, our energy, our love...is eternal.

Love never dies.

Single, Again
June 22
A Love Story

I called my mother on Sunday to wish her a Happy Mother's Day. A few days earlier she woke up and found my father disoriented. She called an ambulance and he has been in the hospital since…no, They have been at the hospital since. She doesn't leave his side. It's crazy how things flip…how when she needed him, he was the caretaker and now every step of the way my mother has become a fierce tiger.

She pauses our conversation to speak to someone who entered the room and then, "Sorry. The nurses just wanted to thank me for helping with dad."

I think of all of the years they have been together, the ups and the downs, the number of times they had to say, "Thank you", or "I'm sorry", or "I need you." We don't come to each other perfect, we arrive imperfect and together figure out the puzzle.

They did that. My parents.

Single, Again
June 23
A very sweet Love Story

They were just barely 21 when they realized they were bringing a baby into this world. She was a college student and he was working hard at a job with a lengthy commute. Neither sure…Who am I? Where am I going? And suddenly the world put a larger question before them. And they answered…. "Yes."

She would come into the world in August. A gorgeous baby with features of hers and the spirit of him. Together they would surround her with the greatest love ever known. She would cuddle her and teach her peaceful ways. He would toss her in the air and make her squeal. She would go from crawling to racing down the beach yelling, "I run!!!!" And we…we would be changed. Their courage would bring out the best in everyone around them. Their faith would make us faithful.

Love would spread like a wildfire…

Single, Again
June 24

I finally finished the sentence, but I am sure more answers will come with time.

There's gonna come a day....
When you are genuinely happy.
When being you is exactly what you want.
When the voice in your head is yours....and only yours.
When shame, insecurity, and embarrassment are only words.
When you wake up and think, what can I do today to make my relationship even better?
When you don't hesitate before you speak.
When you look forward to finding out what happened when you weren't looking.
When you will never again let anyone tell you or make you believe you are not good enough. Because you know you are.
When love will fill you up, and you will give it freely.
When you will live with joy and in gratitude.
There's gonna come a day...for years I heard those words in my head. Randomly popping up, guiding me in faith.

And then, there came the day.... a birthday of sorts. Each a gift to me.
And I love that day.

Single, Again
June 23

Dear God,

This is what I love....

I love all the sounds of the ocean, the rush of the water toward the sand and the crashing of the waves as each drop of water races over the last.

I love the blues of the sky...all of them...the deep, the soft, the bright...and the contrast of the fluffy white clouds against the vastness. I love the stories the clouds tell with their shapes. Shooting stars. Rainbows.

I love babies giggling, the wetness of their lips, the urgency to get everything their little hearts feel, out in a sound. I love crawling. I love soft new dewy skin in pure perfection. Dimples.

I love the end of the day when I change my clothes and climb into my bed like a long-lost friend. Returning to peace, the measurement of time spent...working, playing loving...a cocoon of sheets and blankets.

I love that what hurts, heals. What heals, learns. What learns, becomes. What is, evolves. What evolves, lives.

I love hugging. I love fireworks. I love changing my mind. I love bread...and jelly beans. I love peanut butter.

And God, I love my life.

Single, Again
June 24

Dear 60-year-old me,

Today I am putting my house on the market. You'll remember me sifting through the photos, boxing memories, donating items you hoped would bring happiness and comfort to another. You will see me cleaning, raking, painting, taking trees down, carrying things twice your size and weight up the stairs. Change doesn't just happen. I was never going to be rescued...you know that. Getting the house in order helped you to see what you are capable of and to feel how capable you are.

I walk through the rooms of my home and I can see my children pass through the stages of youth...more good times than bad...more smiles, more successes, more bonding than falling apart. In a box in my closet are my racing medals, a bag of marathon jackets, elementary school pictures, a baby photo of my dad. Symbols of a life well lived.

People will come and walk the halls, measure the rooms, look out the windows, see the structure and wonder. And one family will know...we belong here. And the memories will begin again.

I am thinking of you, 60-year-old me. I am living in the moments of today and carefully walking toward you. When we meet, I am going to take your arm in mine and we are going to go for a walk on the beach. We will laugh about the grandchildren and how wonderful the boys turned out. I will love your wisdom and none of the wrinkles will matter. Only love will really matter.

60-year-old me, I already know that I want to be you.

Love,

51-year-old me

Single, Again
July 4

Dear Mom,

Today I drove away from the house for the last time. Behind me a procession of mini-vans and U-Hauls...cars filled to the brim with things worth keeping. We both know the things worth keeping cried as they walked out...the oldest wrapped around me, his words coming out in waves. "12 years is a long time, mom." As he rides the train back to Boston we text back and forth, all of the things that we needed to say and didn't have time. Each child will need to say goodbye, walk out of his room for the last time. Let go of a place that they called "home". I hope they will look back and smile at the years that get further from us with each passing day.

In the rear view I see all of the things that represent my past. Everything is as it should be. It wasn't easy going through the pictures the kids drew and painted over the years...the photos of trips and sports, the remnants of 25 years. I sat on my driveway, alone, and felt my way through my family history.

Hiding inside those boxes was the realization that I was a really good mom. I decided to pack that deep in my heart.

And bring it with me....

I can't wait until you see my new house. It's exactly what I dreamed of.

Love,
E

Single, Again
July 5

It's just a place, defined by its walls, the landscape, the sky above, a sparkling star, the sound of a river, a lush garden. Things, of course. But they're inanimate and they can only make us feel the things we give them permission to and credit for. She knows that these places have been assigned memories, some she will keep and others she will toss aside. And now, now there is a new place.

The road rolls around the bend, revealing the ocean in all of its majesty. There's a connection of love and happiness to this beach community, a seed of what is about to grow. She has discovered her free self here, found her genuine laugh, her sparkle. The rain that beat against the soil this morning has passed and as she drives closer to her new home, the sun has found its way through the clouds.

The irony of the sun arriving as she does, as if the universe knows to welcome her in the happiest of ways, makes her smile. None of this is lost on her. She knows with every fiber of her being what got her here, who drew her here.

And there he is. Waiting in front of her new house with the keys to everything she has ever wanted.

Single Again
July 7

2018

He ordered two VIP tickets and we met in Cambridge, the room filling up when I arrived. He had been waiting for weeks for this day and was the first to arrive. Three hours early…. Just in time to hold the door for his idol and say, "Good morning, Jack." I've fallen in love with an optimist, a man who hears me gasp at the spot of paint I got on the ceiling and says, "I only see all of the walls you painted right." His mind has given me a soft place to land, his words seal the cracks in my easy to critique mirror. This is his day, and even though I am sick, I would not miss this for the world.

We are in the front row, inches from Jack Canfield and all of his wisdom. I listen to his words, his stories lifting eyebrows, heads nodding, sly smiles, "aha moments." And then we are asked to stand and face a stranger, and my job is to answer this man when he repeatedly asks, "What do you want?"

What do you want? What is your vision for your life, for your love, for your future? I am tripping over my own thoughts, not sure what I really want, or what I need, or what I have the right to ask for. For several minutes he continues to ask, until my guard starts to drop, and I no longer hear my voice through a tunnel. There is only one person who can answer this for me. What do I want?

I want to live on a beach. I want to live in a house that draws my children, my family, my friends, to me. I want walls that are painted the colors of sea glass and a floor that is swept with a broom. I want white curtains blowing in the breeze, and I want a front porch. I want my grandchildren to run from the beach to my home for peanut butter and jelly, and then race back…giggling, my name on their lips as they grab my hands and ask me to play with them. And we will build sandcastles and campfires and memories…lots and lots of memories. And I want to write a book, and it's a New York Times Best Seller. And I see a car pull up to the curb and I climb out and walk to the window and there on a round table is my book. My story.

I look at my stranger and I tell him exactly what I want. I wonder if he listened? I wonder if Jack would be surprised to see me now? Standing here, 8 weeks later, feet in the sand….

Waiting for my grandchildren.

Single, Again
August 14

She wakes up to a fiery ball of pink rising from the edge of the ocean. A new day...a new life...a new chance...and it's all so obvious in this moment. The sound of the waves crashing against the sand, the view from her bed, the breeze off the ocean, the love in her heart...how can this possibly be her life? She runs to her phone and drops back in her bed to capture this moment so that no matter how old she gets, no matter how many sunrises she sees, no matter how long she lives in this home, the glory of her existence never dulls.

She takes a picture and then a video and falls back against her pillow. Her fingers bounce on the keys of her phone as she posts her captured moment, hoping someone, somewhere, will feel and understand what is happening inside her. The healing. The celebrating. The living. The loving.

It's only a place. A building with walls and a roof surrounded by nature. Inanimate objects....

Single, Again
September 19

It's 1988 and I am running down Route 10 lost in thought. I can see kaleidoscopes of color in round discs and it occurs to me that this is exactly how people are. I see me in a bright red and you in a gorgeous yellow, and then we come together…and you change part of me and I change part of you. Suddenly we wonder if we like brown? My thoughts drifted…the brown might work for red but not yellow? And if brown is not good it doesn't mean red and yellow are bad. I saw the colors overlapping and then pulling back and by the end of my run I came to peace with the fact that sometimes relationships don't work out with really good people.

Single, Again
September 20

Sweetheart,

It makes sense that my final letter is to you. There really isn't anything I can tell you that you don't already know. I feel you hear my every thought, in the way that a cloud drifts from one side of the sky to the other...feathery, light, but with purpose. You seem to touch every part of me, effortlessly, as if you were always there even when I couldn't see you.

The last year and a half...it's hard to believe, no? That it isn't longer? It has been a magical transformation for me. I have changed so much that I actually feel like me. You can see the trail of me walking from there to here, shredding the parts of me I no longer needed. The guards, the defense, the fears...I actually think they're gone. Gone. They serve no purpose here but to remind me to continue forward.

Let's always remember the journey. The homes I almost bought, the ones I imagined myself into and you would let us go to, over and over...and try on for size. I was always looking for My home, the one that would seat everyone for Thanksgiving. The one home that my grandchildren would race to. The one home that would make sense of a family that always wanted to feel, really feel, like a family. And you will remember all the times I sat quietly and closed my eyes and thought, "Is this it?" Every vision I had, every dream, you have had with me. And then, like the wind beneath me, you let me do this all in a way that would let me know...I did this!!!

Holy s$@t I did this!!! Even now as I write this, I giggle because I know I could never have gotten here without you. You have this ability to make me feel loved and free at the same time. Encouraged, supported, and believed in. We are the puzzle that fits in the way that others couldn't. The spin of the kaleidoscope that lands on our perfect color, yours blue and mine pink...ours Periwinkle, the color of peace.

I woke up early this morning, before the sun, and I walked through the rooms of my sandcastle, admiring all of the work from the day before. I could run from room to room hugging what is before me. Everything I see, every thought I have, every word I speak becomes part of how I feel. I am surrounded by love.

I climb back into my bed and send you a text. I see the bubbles that let me know that somewhere on the other side of the alphabet, you are thinking of me, and we are both smiling.

This is the story of my journey, of me going back in time to find myself, to heal, to open my heart up again. Mission complete.

I love loving you,
Bella Bella Bella

I turn the page...

My blog had become a friend I could empty my soul to, and ending it wasn't easy. My mission was complete, in that I had found a wonderful man to love. "It's so easy," he likes to say whenever anyone asks how we are. And it is easy, unless we hit a bump and need something to cause us to grow. A bump brought better communication, a bump secured trust, a bump cracked the shell I hid inside.

I left the shell on the beach outside my home. I have no use for it any longer. I look out to the ocean where the swell of the wave forms, rolling toward me, until it crashes at my feet. There is so much energy in the lifting, the peaking of everything the ocean is feeling as it tumbles toward the shore. Over and over the waves repeat their message.

I am here to feel.

After Single, Again
September 25

We went to lunch at Frank Pepe's, which was a surprise to both of us since we were headed to Starbucks for tea. I cherish my time with her. She knew me "before" and then appeared "after". Being her friend makes me feel special, chosen, lucky. We can't wait to sit down and catch up. We focus on each other, she wants to know everything about the house, about my love, my life. And I want to know what's transpired in her tornado-driven life? Walking through the mall, arms bumping on purpose, we joke about how nice it is to sleep alone, not have to hear another person breathe. And then she says, "Until you hear they're not breathing." It becomes so real. She woke up to find him gone, left his body in his sleep, decades before his time.

I ask her if she wants to read some of my new book pages? I pass her my phone and she as she reads, I watch her face, trying to read her thoughts while she reads mine. She looks up and asks, "Do you really think everyone gets this person who is everything you've always wanted?" Her eyes are curious and sad, her lips form a smile.

I wish I could do something to speed her through this process, my petite friend with her curly brown hair and perfect eyelashes. She sits alone in her rowboat, miles from land, the oars dipping in the water one stroke at a time.

It takes more than finding The One. Every day I have to remind myself that what I have needs precious care. I have to think it's everything to make it everything. Our relationship is not making us happy, we are making our relationship happy. Letting go is a conscious release of everything that would ruin this love, letting go is moving forward. "There is free will. Sometimes when he hugs me, I close my eyes and tell myself...Let him love you." And then I melt. It is the first step, finding the one to love. Every step after that determines if it will be "everything you've always wanted."

She shakes her head, I can see in her eyes that she gets it. There is so much more, a greater purpose to our existence than what we see around us. This is just a blip, a very important blip, in time. If you want it, see it, believe it, and make it happen. It isn't random. It's up to you.

After Single, Again
September 26

I never could have written all of this if I had waited until I moved. The lessons are part of me, but the pain has washed away. I didn't realize how being in that home kept so much of it alive, until I left and started again. It was June when I read in my birthday card from my son, "Wherever you are, that's where home is." Go and we will follow.

I lay in my bed and listen to the waves rolling to shore and I realize that the pattern is cleansing me. A year ago, I couldn't even imagine this life. I wake up in the morning to a world that decides even before I realize what's happening, that life is a wondrous journey. The sand, the salt, the colors of the sky and the ocean, the splendor and purity of nature calm me and make me whole.

He meets me at my door and we walk the beach, hand in hand, finding heart shaped rocks and pieces of splintered off colored glass, until he says, "Can we stop for a moment?" We turn and face the ocean to pause. While I am thinking that I can't believe I live here, he stretches out both of his arms and reminds me of what I have accomplished. He had a vision of me before I did. Everything that I ever imagined, and never thought I could achieve, he was certain I would do. He was divinely decided a long time ago, he was made for me. He was made to be the wind beneath me, my dreams and goals. He was made to be the roots to my desires, he was created to be my very best friend. Without hesitation, he breathed life into my soul and reminded me every step of the way. You. Are. Worthy.

If you ask him, he will tell you that I did this all by myself, but I know better. Yes, I prayed for this life. Yes, I dreamed of this home and this man and this happy family. And then one day I woke up and brewed coffee and asked myself where I wanted to have it? For a brief moment I sat in a chair on my porch, but the ocean beckoned me, and my mind said...go. I went to the beach, alone, exhilarated at the discovery. I gave myself permission to be happy. Permission to choose me. I looked behind me and saw only one set of footprints in the sand. I didn't have to look for her any more. 25-year-old me was back where she belonged. Smiling. And that's when I knew.

I had become Bella.

After Single, Again
October 1

He's driving me to the airport and we are sharing intimate details of who we are when no one is looking. The more we share about who we are, the closer we get. The more I know about him the deeper I love him.

"I remember reading when I was young that eating disorders are the strongest sign of self-hate." He nods and says, "Really? Self-hate?"

I can see the beautiful skyline of Boston as we approach the airport. My mind creates the image of a space inside each of us that becomes tarnished by the things we all do that hurt our souls. It's like a basement, but it sits directly in the center of me. If I am honest, I was aware of the dangers of every act of "self-hate" as I did it. I felt the shame and the need for secrecy. I heard the voice in my head that told me I was not where I should be.

I want to go to that place inside me and scrape it clean, and then fill it with his love. And then I want to do the same for him. And fill it with mine.